PATHWAYS TO SUCCESS

Life lessons from global achievers who changed the world

Ordinary to Extraordinary

Part – 1

AspirixWriters
Your Story Starts Here

Dr Rekha & CA Ajay Khandelwal

For permission, contact the publisher:

contact@aspirixwriters.com

Website – https://aspirixwriters.com/

Whatsapp Channel- https://whatsapp.com/channel/0029VbBngx34CrfexYg7f104

ISBN: 978-93-5525-738-3

Edition :2025

Disclaimer

The contents of this book are for inspirational and motivational purposes only. It contains examples from the lives and experiences of achievers around the world. The authors have made every effort to ensure the accuracy of the information presented, but assume no responsibility for any errors or outcomes arising from the use of the information contained herein. Readers are requested to exercise their own judgment and opinions. References to deceased & living individuals are made respectfully and for educational and motivational purposes only.

All photographs used in this book — including those on the cover and inside pages are used under valid Creative Commons (CC) licenses and authorized sources. Proper credit and attribution have been given to each creator or source in accordance with the terms of their respective licenses.

The authors express their sincere gratitude to the photographers, platforms —and other Creative Commons repositories — whose exceptional work has contributed to the visual inspiration of this book.

AspirixWriters

Dedication

To Daaji,

Our Guide and Spiritual Master of Heartfulness

Whose Wisdom and Presence Continually Inspire our journeys, both Within and Outside.

And to our beloved children, Kshitij and Kalpita

whose love, laughter, and dreams fill our hearts with purpose and joy.

You are our true path to success.

Our heartfelt gratitude goes to all those who inspired and supported me in creating this book directly or indirectly.

Table of Contents

Foreword

Pathways to Success is a reminder that extraordinary achievements often begin with ordinary lives—and with the courageous decision to keep moving forward. As I read this book, I was deeply inspired by how beautifully the authors depicted the journeys of successful people around the world who turned failures into fuel and challenges into milestones.

Each story—whether it's Edison's, Steve Jobs's, Jack Ma's, Disney's, or J.K. Rowling's—reveals a powerful truth: success comes to those who believe in themselves, even when the world doesn't. What makes this book truly special is its inclusion of Daaji's teachings, which show that true success isn't just about achieving goals, but also about fostering inner balance, clarity, and peace.

This book isn't just inspiring—it's transformative. It encourages readers to think, dream again, and take meaningful steps toward their own success story. I believe it will help many people transcend limitations and discover the boundless potential within themselves.

With heartfelt appreciation for the author, I invite you to embark on this journey with openness and courage—your story starts with this book….

Amit Khandelwal
Architect | Author | Founder Director, Arch Point Group

Foreword

In every laboratory I've had the opportunity to work in, I've consistently found one thing to be true: scientific progress is never linear. Major discoveries often come only after repeated failures, difficulties, and the lessons learned. Experiments that fail are the ones that show us the path forward.

This book reflects this truth. The success of the people profiled here is not solely due to their accomplishments, but also the challenges they overcame with courage and perseverance. These examples, drawn from diverse fields and countries, demonstrate that success doesn't mean perfection, but rather learning from failure and moving forward.

The special feature of this book is that it showcases humanity alongside success. Behind each story is an ordinary person who decided not to give up in difficult times. In today's world, where success is often portrayed as easy and instant, this book reminds us that true success comes through hard work, learning, and persistent effort.

I am honored to have the opportunity to write the foreword to this inspiring book. I hope it inspires readers to think, learn, and grow.

Dr. Hemant Agarwal
Ph.D. (Germany), Postdoctoral (USA)
Director & Scientist-Flowcytometry Solutions Pvt Ltd, India
www.flowsols.com

From Authors to Readers

– Let's make a new beginning

Dear Reader,

We both believe that there is an untold story of success hidden in every person – all they need is that one spark to ignite and guide them.

Perhaps this is the reason why this book is in your hands.

Because you too want to do something big in your life — and we are with you on this journey. We come from different backgrounds, but our experiences led us to a shared truth — Success does not belong to any particular person; It belongs to every person who believes in himself.

"Pathway to Success" is not just a book, but a guide that shows that anyone can rise above their circumstances. This book is a collection of true stories and life-lessons of people who rose to extraordinary heights from humble beginnings. They did what you can do too –They chose faith over fear, and lessons over stumbling.

We want you to see yourself in each story as you read this book. Every chapter will make you think – "If I change my thinking, can I change my life?" Our answer is – yes, absolutely.

That's the purpose of this book — to remind you that your story isn't over yet, rather, it is starting from here.

In the last chapter of the book, you will meet the deep and simple thinking of “Daaji” – Where success does not just mean achievement, but inner peace and balance. Daaji's teachings remind us that true success is that which stabilizes the mind and satisfies the soul.

This learning has been the turning point of life for both of us. We are not publishing this book for you to “read”, rather want to give “to feel”. Each chapter will awaken the person within you who was silent till now.

And when you turn the last page, we're sure you'll feel a new energy, clarity and confidence within you.

This book is an invitation from us to you –To write your own story, to live your dreams, and to take the first step on your Pathway to Success.

On this journey with you,

Dr. Rekha & CA Ajay Khandelwal

AspirixWriters
WhatsApp channel

Scan the QR Code & Join AspirixWriters

Introduction

Your story starts here

Every person wants to do something big in his life. But most people assume that success is for a select few—those with more opportunity, money, or luck. The truth is that every great achiever was once an ordinary person who made an extraordinary decision – to never give up.

This book, "Pathway to Success," is inspired by the stories of people who rose to extraordinary heights from humble beginnings. They did what we all can do — they changed their mind, and changed their direction.

The purpose of this book is to show you that success is not the property of any one person. This is a path that anyone can follow if they believe in themselves and work hard consistently towards their goals. On this journey there will be mistakes, setbacks, and sometimes the road will seem long. But within these experiences lies the power that changes a person.

In this book you will learn from the lives of people from different corners of the world — some started from small towns, some faced many failures in life, but everyone had one thing in common: they never chose to stop.

You'll learn how they overcame their fears, changed their mindset, and made their mark in the world.

This book is not just an inspiration for you, but a guide. Every chapter contains a new lesson—one that will help you change your thinking, habits, and outlook on life.

You will realize that success is not a destination but a continuous journey. This journey begins when you decide that change is necessary.

Your story starts here - While reading this book, try to see yourself in each story. Ask yourself these questions –

- What do I want to change in my life?
- What can I no longer put off?
- Do I fully realize my potential?

When you honestly look for answers to these questions, you will begin to see your own "Pathway to Success".

Now is the time to start your journey because this book is not just about other people's stories —

This is the beginning of your story.

Chapter 1

Thomas Edison (USA): The Inspiring Journey from Failure to Success

Portrait of Thomas Alva Edison (c.1922), original photo: Library of Congress/Wikimedia Commons (Public Domain) https://commons.wikimedia.org/wiki/File:Thomas_Edison2.jpg

What if your biggest failures are the seeds of world-changing success?

Just imagine: a little boy sits in the corner of his classroom, tears streaming down his face. His teacher calls him "retarded", which means mentally confused and slow. The other children laugh, pointing fingers at the boy who can't grasp even the simplest lesson. That same boy will light up the world in many ways. He will become one of history's greatest inventors.

Here's a twist that will change how you see failure: Thomas Alva Edison didn't succeed despite his struggles, but because of them. Every rejection, every "impossible" claim, every time the world said "give up"—these all sparked a relentless drive that transformed the world of innovation.

If you've ever thought about giving up on your dreams or been told you're not smart, talented or enough —this story is for you. Edison's inspiring journey shows that your struggles today can be the base of your success tomorrow.

The Humble Beginnings of a Future Global Achiever

Thomas Edison's story begins not in a palace or mansion, but in a small brick house in Milan, Ohio, on February 11, 1847. Edison was born in an America trying to find himself. He came into a world where opportunities felt endless, just like the wide-open fields. His parents, Samuel and Nancy Edison were simple folks. Still, they had big dreams for their kid. When Thomas was seven, his family packed their things and moved to Port Huron, Michigan. They were chasing the same dream that inspires countless American families—the hope for better opportunities. Samuel Edison wasn't rich or famous. He was a lighthouse keeper and carpenter. He knew the value of hard work. Nancy Elliott

Edison, a former school teacher, was the most influential person in young Thomas's life.

They had no idea that moving to this small Michigan town would lead to innovations that would change the world. Everyday moments can teach us important lessons. The Edison family's journey for a better life reveals that greatness can emerge from the most surprising situations.

The America of Edison's childhood was a land of dreamers and makers. The Industrial Revolution was speeding up. Railways were connecting distant cities, and inventors were reshaping daily life. Young Thomas was growing up in a time and place where ordinary people made extraordinary things.

But success stories aren't born from comfortable circumstances. They are forged in the fires of adversity, shaped by the very struggles that seem designed to break us. And Edison's greatest challenges were just beginning.

The Struggles That Shaped a Genius

At eight, Thomas Edison experienced a moment that could have broken many kids' spirits for good. His schoolmaster, Reverend G.B. Engle, called him "addled". This meant he was labeled as mentally retarded in front of his classmates. In an era when education was rigorous and unforgiving, this label was devastating. Children who didn’t fit in were often left out. Their potential got hidden under low expectations.

But this is where Edison's success story takes its first incredible turn. His mother, Nancy, refused to give up. She decided to prevent her son from internalizing this painful blow. She pulled Thomas out of school and decided to educate him herself."My mother made me," Edison says. *"She was so genuine, so confident in me, and I felt I had something to live for, someone I shouldn't disappoint."*

> *"My mother made me, she was so genuine, so confident in me, and I felt I had something to live for, someone I shouldn't disappoint."*

Think for a moment about the power of faith. In a world that saw limitations, Nancy Edison saw limitless possibilities. Where others saw a slow child, she recognized a mind that operated in a different way. Her strong faith was the foundation for Edison's empire of innovation.

But the challenges didn't end there. At twelve, Edison started to lose his hearing, and this got worse as he grew older. Most people would have seen this as a tragic disability. Society expected less from those who were different. Many used this to limit their ambitions.

Yet, Edison turned this perceived weakness into his greatest strength. He later said his hearing loss helped him concentrate better. It blocked out distractions that might have taken away his focus. *"My deafness has helped me," he once said*

> *"My deafness has helped me,"*

This is emotional intelligence—the ability to reframe challenges as advantages.

Imagine a teenage Edison as a newspaper boy on the Grand Trunk Railroad, calling out, "Newspaper!" Take your newspaper!" as passengers hurried past. His hearing loss made communication tough. But it also made him more observant and alert to visual cues and patterns. He was developing the very skills that would later make him a master inventor.

The Edison family faced financial struggles during Thomas's youth. Sometimes, putting food on the table felt uncertain. Dreams seemed like a luxury they couldn't afford. Young Edison held different jobs, like selling newspapers and being a telegraph operator. He didn't love these jobs; he did them because his family needed money.

Each job taught him something valuable. Selling newspapers showed him the power of communication and marketing. Working with telegraph equipment introduced him to the mysterious world of electricity. Even during tough times, Edison was unknowingly building the path to his future success.

Edison's early struggles were largely shaped by his relationship with failure. While other inventors kept their work secret until it was flawless, Edison embraced failure as a teacher. His early experiments often ended in disaster—explosions, fires, and destroyed equipment. Yet each failure brought him one step closer to success.

This resilience wasn't personality; it was a life lesson learned out of necessity. Facing adversity as you grow up teaches you to find new ways to overcome obstacles. This builds a strong belief that there's always another path ahead. Edison's struggles weren't just distractions; they were part of his journey to success.

The Making of an Inventor: Curiosity Meets Determination

Edison changed from a struggling young man to a global achiever but it didn't happen overnight. It was created through many hours of testing, deep curiosity, and a strong work ethic that was almost obsessive. What made Edison special wasn't just his intelligence. It was his emotional intelligence and his knack for learning from failures.

In 1868, at the age of 21, Edison received his first patent for an electric vote recorder. He believed this invention would change government processes. It would make voting faster and more accurate. He spent months and a lot of money perfecting the device, sure that success was close.

When he showed his invention to a Massachusetts legislator, he hoped for praise and quick approval. Instead, he got a harsh disappointment. The politician looked at the machine and said, "Young man, this is exactly what we don't want. Your machine will kill the rich American tradition of horse-trading and political games that make legislation engaging."

For many inventors, this rejection would have been the end. The pain of seeing months of work met with such indifference could lead to abandoning the dream.

But Edison's inspiring journey had just begun. He didn't give up. Instead, he learned a key lesson: innovation is just costly experimentation without a market need. *"I don't want to invent anything that won't sell,"* Edison declared after this experience.

> *"I don't want to invent anything that won't sell,"*

This wasn't cynicism; it was wisdom born of failure. He learned to use his creativity to solve real problems that people wanted fixed.

This shift in thinking marked the beginning of Edison's meteoric rise. He moved to New York City, with little money but boundless determination. The city was growing fast, and chances for a clever inventor were all around—if you knew where to look and took risks.

Edison's success came from his work improving the telegraph system. Edison noticed that the Western Union Telegraph Company was facing tech issues. He saw a chance to help. He created a quadraphonic telegraph system. It could send four messages at once over one wire. This doubled the efficiency of his operations.

Edison's story gets really inspiring here: he didn't just improve the telegraph; he struck a deal that changed his life forever.

He didn't sell his invention for a small amount, instead he got Western Union to pay him $40,000, which is over a million dollars today.

Suddenly, the young man who had faced money troubles as a child now had the means to chase his wildest dreams. But money wasn't Edison's ultimate goal; freedom was. Freedom to experiment, freedom to fail, freedom to pursue the impossible.

With this financial support, Edison set up his first real lab in Menlo Park, New Jersey, in 1876. It wasn't a workplace; it was a revolution in how innovation happens. For the first time ever, someone created an "invention factory." This place is made to produce new technologies in a systematic way.

Edison promised to produce "one small invention every ten days and one major one every six months or less." This wasn't an exaggeration; it was confidence based on experience. He learned that innovation relies on both process and perseverance, not just inspiration.

> *"one small invention every ten days and one major one every six months or less."*

The Menlo Park laboratory became the birthplace of over 400 patents. Edison's true genius showed here. He was not just a great inventor, but also a leader. He inspired and coordinated teams of talented people to work together for common goals.

He knew that great achievements need more than just talent. They need teamwork and a common vision.

The Rise of the Phoenix: From Repeated Failures to Historic Successes

Edison's journey to becoming a global achiever had many setbacks. These challenges could have defeated less courageous individuals. Each failure set the stage for a bigger comeback. His resilience became famous the scientific community.

In 1877, Edison was trying to improve Alexander Graham Bell's telephone. During this time, he made an accidental discovery that changed entertainment forever. He tried to record a phone call and ended up making a device that could record sound and play it back. The phonograph was born—humanity's first device capable of reproducing recorded sound.

The impact was immediate and astonishing. When Edison showed the phonograph for the first time, the audience went quiet. Then, they erupted in amazement. Newspapers called it "*the miracle of the age*," and Edison became known as "*The Wizard of Menlo Park.*" At 30 years old, he had achieved what many inventors fail to achieve in a lifetime.

Newspapers called it "*the miracle of the age*," and Edison became known as "*The Wizard of Menlo Park.*"

But Edison's inspiring journey wasn't over yet. His greatest challenge—and his most world-changing success—was still ahead.

The electric bulb wasn't Edison's original idea. Other inventors made early electric lights, but they were not practical. They were too expensive and dangerous. They burned out fast, gave off harsh light, and were not fit for home use. Most experts believed that electric lighting for everyday use was impossible.

Edison saw opportunity where others saw impossibility. His journey to perfect the incandescent bulb is a great example of perseverance despite many failures.

From 1878 to 1879, Edison and his team ran over 3,000 experiments. They were searching for the best. He tried everything—platinum, carbon from various sources, even human hair. Each experiment cost money, time, and energy. Every failure faced criticism from skeptics. They claimed Edison was wasting resources a dream that couldn't succeed.

"Now we know a thousand ways that won't work to make a light bulb," Edison said to his discouraged assistants during a tough time. But instead of viewing these failures as defeats, Edison saw them as invaluable data. Every failed experiment eliminated a possibility and brought him closer to a solution.

> *"I haven't failed. I've just found 10,000 ways that don't work"*

The emotional toll was enormous. Edison worked 18-hour days and slept in his lab. He pushed his body and mind to the limit. His investors were getting impatient. Newspapers were doubting his claims. Meanwhile, competitors raced to solve the same problem. The pressure was crushing.

But this is where Edison's life lessons about resilience became his greatest asset. He learned from a childhood that failures are temporary. He knew that perseverance can help overcome tough obstacles.

His mother's faith in him taught him to believe in himself, even when no one else did.

On October 21, 1879, after testing more than 6,000 different materials, Edison's team made a bulb. They used a carbonized cotton thread filament that lasted for 13.5 hours. It wasn't perfect, but it proved that practical electric lighting was possible.

Success didn't come from divine inspiration. It came from careful experimentation and never giving up. Edison showed that with persistence, creativity, and hard work, even the toughest dreams can come true.

But Edison's vision extended far beyond the creation of a working bulb. He understood that invention was useless without infrastructure. People needed more than just bulbs. They required a whole electrical system including power stations, distribution networks, electric meters, and security systems.

From 1879 to 1882, Edison created the world's first complete electric power distribution system. On September 4, 1882, he flipped a switch at Pearl Street Station in New York City. This brought electric light to 85 customers in lower Manhattan. This was the beginning of the modern electric age.

This success story wasn't just about technology. It was about Edison's skill in seeing the big picture and carrying out a complete vision. While other inventors focused on individual components, Edison was designing an entire industry.

Global Achiever: Transforming the World Through Innovation

By the 1880s, Edison was more than an inventor. He symbolized American innovation and perseverance. His inspiring journey from a rejected schoolboy to a world-changing innovator amazed people everywhere. But his greatest achievements were still ahead.

Edison's motion picture camera, made in 1891, started a whole new kind of entertainment. The Kinetoscope let people watch moving pictures for the first time. This set the stage for the film industry we know today. Edison didn't just invent a device; he imagined a whole industry and made it happen.

His DC (direct current) electrical system was powering cities across America and Europe. Edison's companies made everything from bulbs to power stations. They employed thousands of people and created huge wealth. He had proven that innovation could benefit society and achieve commercial successful.

Edison's biggest contribution may not be one invention. Instead, it was his way of thinking about innovation. The Industrial Research Laboratory he started in Menlo Park set the standard for corporate R&D departments around the world. He organized invention process. He showed that breakthrough innovations could be made consistently with effort and enough resources.

Edison's life lessons extended far beyond technology. He demonstrated that success comes to those who:

Embrace failure as learning: Edison's famous statement, *"I haven't failed. I've just found 10,000 ways that don't work,"* reflects a mindset that views every failure as valuable information rather than defeat.

Keep going beyond what seems possible: When others say something can't be done, truly successful people keep trying. Edison conducted over 3,000 experiments. He wouldn't accept that it couldn't be done.

Think systematically: Edison didn't only create products; he built entire systems and industries. His electrical power grid, movie studios, and research lab showed the strength of big-picture thinking.

Build teams: Edison's greatest innovations came from collaborative efforts. He understood that complex challenges need diverse talents working towards common goals.

Staying in tune with market needs: After failing with the vote recorder, Edison never invented anything that people didn't want.

By 1890, Edison held over 400 patents and his various companies employed over 3,000 people. He had become one of America's most famous and wealthy men, but money was never his primary motivation. *"The value of an idea lies in its use,"* he said, demonstrating that innovation should serve humanity.

"The value of an idea lies in its use"

Edison's workshops and labs became pilgrimage sites for aspiring inventors from around the world.

Young people traveled from Europe, Asia, and across the Americas to see how the *"Wizard of Menlo Park"* worked. He became living proof that in America, anyone with intelligence, perseverance, and creativity can do amazing things.

His success story resonated especially with great impact because of his humble origins. Edison was not born into wealth or privilege. He did not study at prestigious universities or receive elite training. He succeeded because of his curiosity, hard work, and strong belief that creativity and perseverance could solve any problem.

The Man Behind the Legend: Personal Struggles and Human Resilience

Despite his incredible success, Edison's personal life reveals the human side of genius. His first wife, Mary Stilwell, died in 1884 at just 29. This left Edison heartbroken and caring for three young children. The man who could fix the world's tech problems found it hard to handle the emotional issues that affect everyone.

Edison immersed himself in work to cope with grief, often staying in his laboratory for days. His children later felt they had to compete with his inventions for their father's attention. Success, they found, often has personal costs that don't make the headlines.

In 1886, Edison remarried. He found love with Minna Miller, who was 20 years younger. She shared his love for knowledge and similar views on society. Edison's marriage gave him emotional support and a partner who understood his brilliance and humanity.

Edison's inspiring journey also had setbacks that could have defeated those with weaker characters. In the 1890s, he invested a lot in a new iron ore separation process. He thought it would change mining forever. He put a lot of time, energy, and money into this project. He believed it would be his biggest success.

This venture resulted in spectacular failure, costing Edison nearly his entire fortune. Friends and colleagues urged him to file for bankruptcy, give up, and start again with a clean slate. Edison dealt with this setback like he did with all his challenges. He saw it as a learning chance and a way to show his resilience.

"Well, everything's lost, but we had a great time," Edison reportedly told his wife after the iron ore project collapsed. This reaction shows something important about Edison's character: he could separate his identity from his failures. Failure might take his money, but it couldn't shake his confidence or his determination to keep creating.

"Well, everything's lost, but we had a great time"

In a few years, Edison had rebuilt his wealth through other innovations. His storage batteries became widely used in automobiles and industrial applications. His cement company provided materials for some of America's most famous buildings. Even in his 60s and 70s, Edison continued to invent, adapt, and find new ways to add value to the world.

In his later years, Edison showed his dedication to sharing knowledge and inspiring future generations. He became a mentor to countless young inventors, providing advice, resources, and encouragement. *"Genius is one percent inspiration and ninety-nine percent perspiration,"* he said. He stressed that success comes from hard work, not just talent.

> *"Genius is one percent inspiration and ninety-nine percent perspiration"*

His life lessons went beyond invention. They focused on perseverance, optimism, and the belief that smart effort can overcome any obstacle. Edison showed that a child called "dumb" could grow up to light up the world—both in a real and a metaphorical way.

A Legacy That Illuminates the World: Influence and Inspiration

Thomas Edison died on October 18, 1931, at the age of 84, holding 1,093 patents—still a world record. But his true legacy extends far beyond any number. He changed the core aspects of how humans live, work, and entertain themselves.

Consider the scope of Edison's influence on your daily life. The electric light in your home comes directly from Edison's incandescent bulb. The movies you see come from his motion picture camera. The recorded music you listen to exists because Edison invented the phonograph. The electrical power for your appliances comes from systems based on Edison's ideas.

But Edison's most important contribution wasn't technological. It was inspirational. His success shows that amazing things can happen for ordinary people who don't give up. n a world that values talent and luck, Edison showed that hard work and determination can beat tough challenges.

His inspiring journey from a struggling child called "mentally deficient" to the world's top inventor gives hope to those facing tough times. Edison showed that your current situation doesn't define your future. Setbacks can set you up for a comeback. Struggles that feel like defeats can actually build a path to great success.

Modern entrepreneurs and innovators still study Edison's methods. His method of systematic experimentation, team building, and market-focused innovation is still relevant today. This is true even in the age of Silicon Valley startups and tech disruption.

Innovation at companies like Apple, Google, and Tesla comes from their industrial research labs. These labs trace their roots back to Edison's Menlo Park.

Edison's life lessons continue to inspire those facing their own challenges.

When others doubt you, trust yourself: Edison was called "retarded" as a child, but he became one of history's top inventors. Outside opinions don't define your potential.

Turn disadvantages into advantages: Edison's hearing loss became a tool for concentration. Your greatest struggles may contain the seeds of your greatest strengths.

Embrace failure as a chance to learn: Edison's 10,000 failed bulb experiments weren't just failures. They showed him what didn't work and led him closer to success.

Think beyond personal success: Edison didn't just make products; he built systems, industries, and chances for others. True success elevates others just as it elevates you.

Keep learning and adapting: Edison kept innovating into his 80s. This shows that curiosity and growth can last a lifetime.

Edison's story reminds us that success isn't about avoiding failure—it's about persevering through failure until you achieve success. His inspiring journey shows that with perseverance, creativity, and a willingness to learn from setbacks, anyone can shine bright in the world.

Your Turn to Light Up the World: Interactive Challenges and Life Lessons

Edison's success story isn't just history. It's a guide for your journey, showing how to move from where you are now to where you want to be. The same ideas that turned a rejected schoolboy into a global star can also change your life today.

But inspiration without action is mere entertainment. Edison once said, "Vision without execution is hallucination." So, let's turn his lessons into practical steps you can take today.

> *"Vision without execution is hallucination."*

Challenge 1: Reframe Your Failures

Edison famously said he "discovered 10,000 ways that didn't work" before he perfected the bulb. Which "failures" in your life can you reframe as valuable learning experiences?

Take a moment right now and think about a recent failure or disappointment. Instead of asking *"Why did this happen to me?"*, ask *"What did it teach me?"* Write down three specific lessons from that experience. Edison would say it's not just positive thinking. It's strategic thinking that gets you ready for success in the future.

Challenge 2: Identify your "retard" labels

People called Edison "retard" as a child—a devastating label that could define his entire life. What negative labels have others placed on you? "Not smart enough." "Too old." "Wrong background." "Not talented."

Make a list of these labels, then next to each, write evidence that refutes them. Edison's mother saw genius where others saw limitations. You must become your own advocate, your own confidant, your own source of unwavering faith.

Challenge 3: Find your Menlo Park

Edison built the first industrial research lab. He knew that major innovations need special space, time, and focused work. Where is your "laboratory" to pursue your dreams?

This doesn't have to be a physical location (although it can be). It could be a specific time each day to learn new skills. It might be a group of people who share your vision. Or, it could just be a promise to keep working toward your goals. The key is intentionality—creating conditions that support your growth and innovation.

Challenge 4: Build Your Innovation System

Edison didn't invent by chance. He made clear steps to find problems, test solutions, and launch products. What systematic approach can you develop to achieve your goals?

Break your biggest dream into small, manageable experiments. Create a program to test new approaches. Develop metrics to measure progress. Edison's success came from seeing innovation as a discipline, not just inspiration.

Challenge 5: Adopt a long-term mindset

Edison spent more than a year doing thousands of experiments to perfect the light bulb. In our culture of instant gratification, such perseverance seems almost supernatural. But Edison knew that meaningful achievements need sustained effort over time.

If you had committed to it and worked on it consistently for five years, what would you have achieved? Edison's inspiring journey shows us that time is often the most overlooked key to success. Consistent effort over time leads to results that feel hard to achieve quickly.

Reflection Questions for Deeper Thinking:

1. What impossible dream would you pursue if you knew you couldn't fail? Edison's bulb seemed impossible until it happened. Your "impossible" dream probably requires more experimentation and perseverance.

2. How can your biggest struggle become your greatest strength? Edison's hearing loss helped him concentrate better.

What challenge in your life might actually be preparing you for future success?

3. What could you have achieved if you hadn't worried so much about what others think? Edison continued to invent despite critics, skeptics, and setbacks. How would your life change if you didn't let others' opinions hold you back?

4. What problem in the world bothers you so much that you'd be willing to work for years to solve it? Edison's best inventions addressed real problems that improved people's lives. Lasting success comes from creating value for others.

5. What would you strive for if you had Edison's perseverance? That man conducted over 50,000 experiments in his lifetime. What could you achieve with that level of consistent effort?

Your personal success story begins now.

Edison's inspiring journey from failure to success didn't happen by accident. He succeeded because he made specific choices each day. He kept experimenting when others quit. He saw chances where others saw problems. He persevered, even when it felt pointless.

You have a similar choice available to you right now. You can accept what others say you can't do, or you can follow Edison's lead and believe that nothing worthwhile is impossible.

You can let setbacks defeat you, or you can use them—like Edison—as sources of information.

The world needs what you have to offer. There are problems only you can solve, innovations only you can create, and value only you can deliver. Edison showed that ordinary people can do amazing things. But they must be ready to work very hard for a long time.

Your inspiring journey starts with one decision: Will you let failures hold you back, or will you, like Edison, keep trying until you succeed?

The choice is yours. The time is now. The world is waiting.

What will you invent? What problems will you solve? What light will you bring into the darkness?

Edison's success story is proof that it is possible. Your success story is waiting to be written.

There's only one question: Are you ready to begin?

.

Chapter 2

Steve Jobs (USA) – The Visionary Who Changed the World

Photo: Matthew Yohe / CC BY 3.0 Unported / Wikimedia Commons – https://commons.wikimedia.org/wiki/File:Steve_Jobs_with_MacBook_Air.jpg

Would you be surprised to know that one of the world's top innovators was once seen as a "college dropout" with no clear path?

Imagine this picture: a young man, just 20, sits in his Reed College dorm, questioning everything around him. The expensive fees were eating into his adoptive parents' savings, but the classes felt pointless. So, he made a decision that shocked everyone – he dropped out. That was young Steve Jobs. This choice set the stage for one of the most inspiring journeys ever, moving from failure to success.

When you swipe your iPhone, listen to music on your iPad, or admire a MacBook's design, you feel the impact of a man who wouldn't settle for ordinary. Steve Jobs's journey to success wasn't easy. It was marked by rejection and failure. Still, he held a strong belief that he could change the world.

The Early Seeds of Greatness

Steve Jobs was born on February 24, 1955, in San Francisco. His story starts with a struggle that influenced his quest for perfection. His biological parents couldn't care for him, so they had to make the tough choice to give him up for adoption. Paul and Clara Jobs, a mechanic and an accountant, welcomed Steve into their small home in Mountain View, California. This area later became known as Silicon Valley.

Right from the start, Steve was different. While other kids played with toys, he was drawn to the electronics in his adoptive father's garage. Paul Jobs had rough hands and a patient nature. He spent hours teaching Steve. They worked on opening radios, rebuilding engines, and understanding the complex mechanisms behind how things work.

Can you think about what a young child feels when he takes something apart for the first time and sees what's inside? Steve Jobs' future innovations came from his curiosity and his endless questions of "why" and "how."

"What I learned in that garage, I could never learn in any classroom," Jobs would say later, his voice warm with genuine gratitude.

> *"What I learned in that garage, I could never learn in any classroom"*

But school? School was a completely different story. Young Steve found traditional education stifling. His sharp mind craved excitement, creativity, and challenges that his teachers just couldn't offer. People knew him as a mischievous kid, someone who questioned everything and everyone.

Teachers saw his great intelligence and suggested dropping some classes. But Paul and Clara worried about their son's social growth. So, they chose to keep him with kids his own age. This decision proved crucial. Steve didn't rush through school. Instead, he found new ways to focus his energy.

In high school, he joined the Explorer's Club at Hewlett-Packard. There, he got his first real taste of the computer world. The seeds of his future were being planted, one circuit board at a time.

The College Years: The Search for Meaning

In 1972, Steve enrolled at Reed College in Portland, Oregon. But it was here that his inspiring journey took an unexpected turn. After one semester, he realized something shocking: he was wasting his parents' hard-earned money on an education that didn't teach him what he wanted to learn.

So, he did the unthinkable — he dropped out of college.

But Steve Jobs wasn't giving up; he was just getting started. Instead of leaving campus altogether, he became what he called a "drop-in." He slept on friends' dorm floors, returned Coke bottles for money, and chose classes that really interested him.

One of these classes was a course in calligraphy taught by a Trappist monk. The course introduced Steve to the beauty of typography, spacing, and design. It felt pointless back then, but it laid the groundwork for his most groundbreaking discoveries later.

"If I hadn't taken that course in college, the Mac wouldn't have had multiple typefaces or proportionally spaced fonts," Jobs later told Stanford students in his famous 2005 speech.

> *"If I hadn't taken that course in college, the Mac wouldn't have had multiple typefaces or proportionally spaced fonts"*

He filled this period of his life with uncertainty and self-discovery. He went to India in search of spiritual enlightenment but returned seven months later. Now he was thinner, sicker, and more confused than before. He experimented with meditation, vegetarianism, and different philosophies. To outsiders he might have thought he was lost. But Steve Jobs was actually finding himself.

Early Failures: The Making of a Visionary

After returning from India, Steve took a job at the Atari video game company. But success didn't come easily here either. His co-workers found him arrogant and difficult to work with. His hygiene was poor, his attitude was rude, and his ideas were often dismissed. Eventually he was moved to the night shift so his co-workers didn't have to deal with him during regular hours.

Can you imagine? The future CEO of one of the world's most valuable companies was working alone at night because people couldn't stand being around him during the day. But here's what's remarkable about Steve Jobs' story: He used every rejection, every criticism, and every failure as fuel for his ambition.

"My favorite things in life cost nothing. It's quite clear that the most precious resource we have is time," he would later say, realizing that these early struggles weren't setbacks but preparation for his future success.

> *"My favorite things in life cost nothing. It's quite clear that the most precious resource we have is time"*

During this time, Steve rekindled his friendship with Steve Wozniak, a brilliant engineer who shared his passion for electronics. Wozniak had created something extraordinary—a personal computer that was smaller, more accessible, and more user-friendly than anything else on the market. But Wozniak was content to share his invention with friends at the local computer club.

Steve Jobs saw something different. He saw the future.

Breakthrough Moment: The Birth of Apple

On April 1, 1976, Apple Computer Company was officially founded in the Jobs family's now-famous garage. But it was no fairy-tale beginning. Steve had to sell his most cherished possession, his Volkswagen bus, to raise the capital for his first order. Wozniak sold his HP calculator. All he had was $1,300 and a dream most people thought was impossible.

His first product, the Apple I, was basically an assembled circuit board that computer enthusiasts could use to build their own machines. He sold it for $666.66 - not because of any sinister meaning, but because Wozniak loved repeating digits, and it represented a 33% markup on his costs.

But Steve Jobs wasn't thinking small. Where others were looking at a hobbyist product, he envisioned computers in every home, school, and office. When he developed the Apple II, he emphasized something revolutionary for its time—a sleek plastic case that made the computer accessible to everyday consumers, not just tech enthusiasts.

"We wanted to make a computer so user-friendly that people didn't have to think about how it worked," Jobs explained, his eyes shining with the passion that would define his career.

> *"We wanted to make a computer so user-friendly that people didn't have to think about how it worked"*

The Apple II was a phenomenal success. Sales grew 700% year over year. When Apple went public in 1980, the company was valued at $1.2 billion, the largest IPO in history up to that time. Steve Jobs was 25 years old and worth over $200 million.

But success, as Steve was about to discover, can be just as challenging as failure.

The Downfall: Exile from Your Own Kingdom

Success breeds confidence, and confidence can breed arrogance. By the early 1980s, Apple had transformed from a two-person startup into a major corporation with thousands of employees. Steve Jobs, still in his twenties, struggled to manage not only products but also people. His perfectionist tendencies, which had driven Apple's innovation, were now causing friction within the company.

The situation reached a peak with the launch of the Macintosh in 1984. While the Mac was a technological marvel—the first large-scale computer with a graphical user interface—it was also expensive and initially struggled in the market. Internal tensions grew, and the board of directors began to question Steve's leadership abilities.

In 1985, after a failed boardroom coup, Steve Jobs faced the most devastating moment of his career. The company he had built from scratch, the very name he had chosen, ousted him. At the age of 30, Steve Jobs was essentially fired from Apple.

Imagine what must have gone through his mind at that time? The company he considered his baby, the one he had given everything to, was telling him he was unwanted.

"I didn't see it then, but it turned out that being fired from Apple was the best thing that could have happened to me," he later reflected. *"The weight of being successful was replaced by the lightness of being a beginner again, less certain about everything. It freed me to enter the most creative period of my life."*

"I didn't see it then, but it turned out that being fired from Apple was the best thing that could have happened to me"

But in that moment, it didn't feel like freedom. It felt like failure. Complete, public, humiliating failure.

The Wilderness Years: Building New Dreams

What do you do when your life's work rejects you? Most people might retreat, become bitter, or give up altogether. But Steve Jobs wasn't most people. Instead of dwelling on his rejection, he channeled his energy into creating something new.

He founded NeXT Computer, a company that focused on high-end workstations for the business and education markets. The computers were beautiful, powerful, and incredibly expensive. They were also commercial failures. NeXT sold only 50,000 machines in its entire 12-year existence.

Additionally, Steve made another investment that seemed like a big bet at the time. He bought Lucasfilm's computer graphics division for $10 million and transformed it into Pixar Animation Studios. For years, Pixar struggled to find its identity, losing money while creating computer graphics for commercials and short films.

During this period, Steve faced some of the darkest moments of his career. NeXT was struggling, Pixar was burning cash, and many in Silicon Valley dismissed him as a once-lucky man. The pressure was immense, and there were times when he questioned whether he had made the right choices.

But then, something magical happened.

Renaissance: The Return of the King

In 1995, Pixar released "Toy Story," the world's first fully computer-animated feature film. It became an instant hit, grossing over $374 million worldwide and establishing Pixar as a major player in Hollywood. The company went public the same week the film was released, and Steve Jobs became a billionaire for the first time.

But the real turning point came in 1997, when Apple acquired NeXT for $429 million. As part of the deal, Steve Jobs returned to the company he co-founded 21 years earlier—initially not as CEO, but as an advisor. However, within months, he had established himself back at the top position.

The Apple Steve returned to was very different from the one he left. The company was on the verge of bankruptcy, with only 90 days of cash left. Market share had plummeted, and many analysts were suggesting Apple should simply shut down and return whatever money it had to shareholders.

"We have to go back to basics," Steve told his team. His first move was dramatic and decisive: he eliminated nearly 70% of Apple's products, focusing the company on just four categories: desktop computers and laptops for both consumers and professionals.

Then came the products that were going to change everything.

A Decade of Innovation: Changing the World, One Product at a Time

The late 1990s and 2000s saw one of the most remarkable innovation series in business history. Under Steve Jobs' leadership, Apple didn't just make products; they created entirely new categories of technology that transformed the way we live, work, and communicate.

iMac (1998): Making Computers Beautiful
The first sign of Apple's comeback came with the iMac, an all-in-one computer that looked different from anything else on the market. Available in translucent colors like Bondi Blue, the iMac made technology accessible and fun. *"It looks good enough to lick,"* Steve said with characteristic confidence.

> *"It looks good enough to lick"*

The iMac sold 800,000 units in its first five months, single-handedly saving Apple from bankruptcy and announcing to the world that the company was back in the innovation game.

iPod (2001): Music in Your Pocket

"1,000 songs in your pocket." That's how Steve Jobs introduced the iPod, a device that would revolutionize not only Apple but the entire music industry. When most portable music players were clunky and difficult to use, the iPod was brilliant, intuitive, and addictive.

> *"1,000 songs in your pocket."*

But Steve didn't stop there. In 2003, Apple launched the iTunes Store, creating a legal way for people to buy and download music. It sold over a million songs in its first week, proving that people will pay for content if the experience is seamless and convenient.

iPhone (2007): A Phone, an iPod, and an Internet Communicator

On January 9, 2007, Steve Jobs walked onto the stage of the Macworld Convention & Expo in San Francisco and gave what many consider the greatest product presentation in business history. He introduced three revolutionary products: a widescreen iPod with touch controls, a revolutionary mobile phone, and a breakthrough Internet communication device.

Then he revealed that these weren't three separate devices—it was one device. The iPhone.
"Today, Apple is going to reinvent the phone," he declared, and he wasn't exaggerating. The iPhone didn't just compete with existing smartphones; it created an entirely new category. With its multi-touch interface, app ecosystem, and seamless integration of multiple functions, the iPhone transformed not only apple but the entire technology landscape.

"Today, Apple is going to reinvent the phone," he declared, and he wasn't exaggerating.

Within two years, the iPhone was generating more revenue than the entire iPod business. By 2011, it accounted for more than half of Apple's profits.

iPad (2010): Creating a New Category

Not content with revolutionizing phones and computers, Steve had a vision to create an entirely new category of device. The iPad, launched in 2010, was designed to bridge the gap between smartphones and laptops. Critics initially dismissed it as "just a bigger iPhone," but consumers quickly embraced it.

The iPad sold 300,000 units on its first day and three million in its first 80 days. This created the tablet computer market overnight and once again established Apple as a major player in another technology category.

The Philosophy Behind the Magic

During this incredible innovation spree, Steve Jobs operated according to a set of principles that set Apple apart from every other technology company. These weren't just business strategies; they were deeply held beliefs about how technology should serve humanity.

Simplicity as the Ultimate Sophistication

"*Simple can be harder than complex,*" Steve often said. *"You have to work hard to clear your thinking to simplify. But it's worth it in the end because once you get there, you can move mountains."*

> *"Simple can be harder than complex"*

This philosophy drove every aspect of Apple's design process. Where competitors added features, Apple subtracted them. Where others created complex user manuals, Apple designed products that were intuitive from the moment you touched them.

Perfectionism as a Driving Force

Steve Jobs was renowned for his attention to detail. He would delay product launches if a curve wasn't exactly right, if a color was a shade off, or if the packaging didn't evoke the right emotional response. This perfectionism frustrated employees and partners, but it also created products that competitors couldn't match.

"*We don't get the chance to do so many things, and everyone has to be truly excellent,*" he explained. "*Because this is our life. Life is brief, and then you die, you know? And we all chose to do this with our lives. So, it has to be great. It has to be worth it.*"

"*We don't get the chance to do so many things, and everyone has to be truly excellent*"

The Intersection of Technology and the Liberal Arts

Unlike many tech leaders who focused purely on engineering and specifications, Steve believed that the most powerful innovations occurred at the intersection of technology and the liberal arts. This philosophy, rooted in his liberal arts education and calligraphy studies, led to products that were not only functional but also emotionally resonant.

"It's in Apple's DNA that technology alone is not enough," he said during one of his famous keynote presentations. "It's technology, married to the liberal arts, married to the humanities, that produces results that make our hearts sing."

The Darkest Hour: The Fight for Life

In 2003, at the height of Apple's renaissance, Steve Jobs received devastating news. Doctors had discovered a tumor in his pancreas—pancreatic cancer, one of the most aggressive and deadly forms of the disease. Most people with pancreatic cancer do not live longer than a year.

Steve initially resisted conventional treatment, preferring dietary changes and alternative medical approaches. Only nine months later did he consent to surgery. The delay may have cost him precious time, but it also reflected his lifelong belief that he could control his own destiny through willpower and perseverance.

Even while battling cancer, Steve continued to drive Apple's innovation forward. He oversaw the development of the iPhone and iPad while taking treatments that left him weak and thin. His dedication to the company never wavered, even as his health deteriorated.

In 2005, he delivered one of the most famous commencement speeches in history at Stanford University. Thin from cancer treatment but still impressive in his presence, he shared three stories from his life and concluded with words that inspired millions:

"Your time is limited, so don't waste it living someone else's life. Don't fall into the trap of dogma—which is living with the results of another people's thinking. Don't let the noise of other people's opinions drown out your inner voice. And most importantly, have the courage to follow your heart and intuition. They somehow already know what you really want to become. Everything else is secondary."

The Final Chapter: A Legacy Beyond Products

On October 5, 2011, Steve Jobs passed away at his home in Palo Alto, California. He was 56 years old. The news sent shockwaves around the world as millions realized they had lost not just a CEO but a visionary who had fundamentally changed their daily lives.

Within hours of the announcement, Apple Stores around the world became unofficial memorial sites. People left flowers, apples, Post-it note tributes, and iPad displays showing photos and messages. This outpouring of grief wasn't just for a business leader—it was for someone who had touched their lives in deeply personal ways.

But Steve Jobs' true legacy wasn't billions of dollars in revenue, revolutionary products, or even transforming Apple into the world's most valuable company. His legacy was proof that one person, armed with vision, perseverance, and an unwavering belief in their own ability to change the world, could indeed change the world.

Life Lessons from a Revolutionary

Steve Jobs' inspiring journey from college dropout to global icon offers profound life lessons that extend far beyond business and technology:

Embrace your failures as preparation for success

Every major setback in Steve's life—dropping out of college, being fired from Apple, the initial failures of NeXT—became the foundation for his greatest achievements. He understood that failure isn't the opposite of success; it's a necessary part of it. *"I believe that about half of what separates successful entrepreneurs from non-successful ones is pure perseverance,"* he once said. When you face rejection or failure, remember that you're not being held back—you're being prepared for something better.

> *"I believe that about half of what separates successful entrepreneurs from non-successful ones is pure perseverance"*

Follow your curiosity, even if it doesn't make sense

Steve's decision to attend a calligraphy class seemed absurd at the time, but it directly influenced Mac's revolutionary typography. His spiritual journey to India didn't provide the answers he was looking for, but it taught him about simplicity and focus. Trust that your interests and experiences will connect in ways you can't predict.

Don't let others determine your worth

When Apple fired Steve Jobs, many dismissed him as a failure. He could have accepted their decision and faded into obscurity. Instead, he used their rejection as motivation to prove them wrong. Your failures don't define you—your comeback does.

Perfection is a process, not a destination

Steve Jobs was famous for his obsession with perfecting every detail, but he understood that perfection wasn't about being flawless—it was about continuous improvement. Every Apple product went through dozens of prototypes and iterations. Excellence comes from refining your work until it couldn't be better.

Build something bigger than yourself

Steve's ultimate goal wasn't wealth or fame—it was to create products that improved people's lives. When you focus on serving others rather than yourself, success becomes a natural byproduct of your contribution.

The Ongoing Revolution

Today, more than a decade after Steve Jobs' passing, his influence continues to shape our world. Apple, one of the most valuable companies worldwide, continues to innovate in ways that honor his vision. But more importantly, his story continues to inspire entrepreneurs, creators, and dreamers around the world who believe they, too, can change the world.
The technologies we use daily—touchscreen interfaces, app ecosystems, cloud computing, wireless earbuds—all bear the marks of the innovations that Steve Jobs either pioneered or perfected. But perhaps his greatest innovation was proving that technology can be both powerful and beautiful, functional and emotional.

In a world that often seems dominated by cynicism and limitations, Steve Jobs' life is a testament to the power of unwavering optimism. He believed that a small team of passionate people could change the world, and he spent his life proving this belief true.

Your Turn: Questions for Reflection and Action

As we end this inspiring journey through Steve Jobs' life, take a moment to consider how his lessons might apply to your own aspirations:

Questions for Reflection:

1. What "calligraphy class" in your life — something you're drawn to that doesn't seem practical — might be preparing you for your future? Steve's seemingly irrelevant typography studies were at the heart of the revolutionary design of the Mac.

2. When were your biggest failures actually preparing you for later success?How might your current challenges be preparing you for something even bigger? Remember, Steve's exile from Apple led to NeXT and Pixar — experiences that made him a better leader.

3. If you had unlimited resources and knew you couldn't fail, what would you create or change in the world? It's not just dreaming — it's identifying the vision that could drive your life's work.

4. What skills or experiences do you have that together could create something unique and valuable? Innovation often happens at the intersection of different fields and disciplines.

5. How could you simplify something complex in your field to make it more accessible to others? Steve's genius was in making sophisticated technology feel intuitive and easy.

6. Who are the "top performers" in your life, and how can you spend more time with people who elevate your thinking and standards? Excellence is contagious—surround yourself with it.

7. What story does your current work tell about you and your values? Every project, every conversation, every decision helps reveal who you are becoming.

8. Where in life do you settle for "good enough" when you could strive for excellence? Identify an area where raising your standards could change your results.

9. What conventional wisdom in your field should be challenged? The greatest opportunities often lie in challenging the things everyone takes for granted.

10. If you knew you had limited time (as we all do), what would be your top priority? Steve's awareness of mortality focused his energy on the things that truly matter.

Action Challenges:

1. 30-Day Curiosity Challenge: For the next 30 days, spend 30 minutes a day learning about something that interests you but seems relevant to your career. Notice what connections emerge.

2. Simplicity Challenge: Choose an area of your life that feels complicated or cluttered. Use Steve Jobs' philosophy of simplicity and remove everything that doesn't matter.

3. Practice Perfectionism: Instead of striving for perfection, focus on improving one thing by 1% every day. Track your progress over time.

4. Vision Statement: Write a one-sentence description of the change you want to make in the world. Post it somewhere you can see it daily.

5. Rejection Archive: Record the next five "nos" or rejections you receive. Later, reflect on how each one led you to better opportunities.

Final Words: Your Story Awaits You

Steve Jobs once said, *"Those who are crazy enough to think they can change the world are the ones who will change the world."* As you close this chapter and return to your life, remember that everyone who changed the world started where you are—with a vision, a little doubt, and the courage to take the first step.

> *"Those who are crazy enough to think they can change the world are the ones who will change the world."*

Your inspiring journey has just begun. The world is waiting for your unique contribution that only you can make. The question isn't whether you can achieve great things—Steve Jobs' story proves that anyone can achieve extraordinary things. The question is: what will you do with the life you've been given?

The future is calling. The time to respond is now.

"Innovation distinguishes between a leader and a follower. The question is: which one will you choose to be?" - Steve Jobs

> *"Innovation distinguishes between a leader and a follower. The question is: which one will you choose to be?"*

Chapter 3

Jack Ma (China) – From 30 Rejections to Billionaire Visionary

Photo: World Economic Forum / CC BY-SA 3.0 Unported / Wikimedia Commons – https://commons.wikimedia.org/wiki/File:Jack_Ma_2008.jpg retrieved on 27th sept. 2025

What if I told you that the man who built the world's largest e-commerce empire was rejected from 30 jobs...even from KFC?

Visualize this: A skinny young man walks into a KFC restaurant in Hangzhou, China. Twenty-four other people are applying for the same job. Twenty-three get the job, but he doesn't. The reason? *"You don't look good enough,"* they said. This same man would later build a company worth over $400 billion and become one of the most influential business leaders in the world.

His name is Jack Ma, and his inspiring journey from repeated rejection to global success will shatter every excuse you've ever made for not achieving your dreams.

But what makes Jack's story truly special is this: He didn't just overcome failure—he collected them like trophies. He was rejected from university twice. He applied to Harvard Business School ten times and was rejected each time. When the internet arrived in China, no one believed his vision. When he started Alibaba, investors laughed at him.

Yet today, Singles Day—his creation—earns more in 24 hours than Black Friday and Cyber Monday combined. His story isn't just a success story; it's a masterclass in turning rejection into rocket fuel for success.

Are you ready to learn how the man who couldn't get a job at KFC built an empire that employs over 250,000 people worldwide? Let's dive into this incredible story that proves that your current circumstances have nothing to do with your final destination.

The Boy Who Dreamed in English

Born on September 10, 1964, in Hangzhou, China, Jack Ma Yun came into this world during one of the most challenging periods in Chinese history. His family lived just above the poverty line—

his grandfather was labeled a "rightist" during the Cultural Revolution, making life extremely difficult for the entire family.

But this is where Jack's story becomes fascinating: while other children his age were playing with toys he couldn't afford, Jack was pursuing something that seemed equally impossible—learning English.

Why English? Because young Jack had noticed something magical happening in his city. Foreign tourists were beginning to visit Hangzhou's beautiful West Lake, and he realized that speaking their language could open doors for him to worlds he had never imagined.

So, what did this determined child do? Every morning at 5 a.m., while his peers were still asleep, Jack would cycle to the Shangri-La Hotel. He would approach foreign visitors and offer them a tour of the city—for free—just for the chance to speak English.

Imagine this scene: a skinny Chinese boy, barely reaching the shoulders of these tall foreigners, enthusiastically recounts the history of ancient temples and beautiful gardens, stumbling over words but never giving up. Tourists loved his passion and energy. They began inviting him over for dinner, teaching him not just English but also about the wider world beyond China's borders.

This is your first life lesson from Jack Ma: When you can't afford formal education, create your own. When opportunities don't come your way, go and find them. When you want something badly enough, you will find a way—even if it means waking up at 5 a.m. every day for nine years.

> *When you can't afford formal education, create your own. When opportunities don't come your way, go and find them.*

Yes, you read that right. Jack did this for nine years. Even in rain, snow, and scorching heat. His dedication to learning English wasn't just about the language—it was about developing the tenacity and resilience that would later build an empire.

A beautiful irony? Those morning conversations with tourists weren't just teaching him English—they were teaching him how to connect with people from different cultures, how to build trust quickly, and how to convey big ideas simply. All of these skills would prove invaluable later when he pitched Alibaba to international investors.

A University of Harsh Realities

Jack's first real taste of systematic rejection came when he tried to get into university. The Gaokao—China's notoriously difficult college entrance exam—shattered his dreams not once, but twice.

First attempt: Failed miserably in math. The score was so low that it was embarrassing.

Second attempt: Failed again. This time, his math score was slightly better, but still nowhere near passing.

Most people would have given up. Society expected him to accept his fate and find menial work. But Jack had learned something from those years of meeting strangers in hotels: Perseverance beats talent when talent lacks perseverance.

Third attempt: Finally, he passed, but barely. He was admitted to Hangzhou Teachers' Institute (now Hangzhou Normal University)—not quite Harvard, but a ticket to higher education.

What I love most about this part of Jack's story: He didn't just make it through college. He put his heart and soul into everything—student government, organizing events, learning, growing. He understood that success doesn't come from where you start; it comes from what you do with the opportunities you receive.

After graduating in 1988, Jack became an English teacher, earning $12 a month. Twelve dollars! But even in this humble position, his leadership qualities shone through. His students loved him because he didn't just teach English—he taught them to dream big, to believe in possibilities far greater than their current circumstances.

A pattern was already forming: Jack Ma possessed the extraordinary ability to see potential where others saw only limitations, to inspire hope where others saw only obstacles. This $12-a-month teacher was already demonstrating qualities that would later inspire thousands of employees and millions of small business owners worldwide.

The Olympics of Rejection

If rejection were an Olympic sport, Jack Ma would have won numerous gold medals. After his teaching career, he decided to enter the business world. What followed was a masterclass in perseverance that should be essential learning for anyone pursuing their dreams.

These statistics are astonishing:

- Applied for 30 different jobs: Rejected by all 30
- Applied to be a police officer: Rejected (said to be too weak)
- Applied to Harvard Business School: Rejected 10 times
- When KFC came to China, 24 people applied for the job: 23 got it, Jack didn't

But the most interesting rejection was this: When Jack first discovered the internet during a business trip to the US in 1995, he was absolutely mesmerized. He searched for "beer" and found beer from every country except China. He searched "China" and found almost nothing.

Returning to China, he tried to convince government officials and business leaders of the internet's potential. Their response? **They thought he was crazy.**

"The internet? What good will it do? China isn't ready for this technology."

"Young man, you're living in fantasy. Focus on real business."

Even his wife initially thought he was losing his mind.

But this is where Jack Ma's true character truly came to the fore: instead of being discouraged by rejections, he began to accumulate them. He began to view every "no" not as a closing door, but as valuable market research. Each rejection taught him something about people's fears, market readiness, and the right timing.

Jack's philosophy during this time: *"If you don't give up, you still have a chance. Giving up is the biggest failure."*

> *"If you don't give up, you still have a chance. Giving up is the biggest failure."*

A First Glimpse of the Internet's Magic

In 1995, Jack traveled to the United States as part of a small delegation. This trip not only changed his life, but also transformed the entire landscape of Chinese business.

When his American friend first showed him, a computer connected to the Internet, Jack was skeptical. *"What can this machine do?"* he asked.

His friend suggested they search for something. Jack said "beer." Within seconds, the screen filled with information about beer from Germany, Japan, and the United States—everywhere except China.

Then they searched for "China." Almost nothing came up.

In that moment, Jack saw something that would haunt him for the next decade: China—a country of over a billion people—was virtually invisible on the Internet. This wasn't just a business opportunity; it was a chance to connect China to the world, and the world to China.

But when he returned to China and tried to explain this vision, people looked at him as if he were speaking a different language. The Internet was still this mysterious, foreign concept. Most people had never even seen a computer.

Jack's answer? He still started his first Internet company.

Internet Pioneer (Somewhat)

In 1995, Jack and his wife invested all their savings—a total of $1,000—to start China Pages, one of China's first internet companies. The idea was simple: build websites for Chinese companies so they could showcase their products online.

The problem? Almost no one in China knew what a website was, let alone why they might need one.

Imagine Jack trying to explain the internet to potential customers in 1995:

"So, Mr. Chen, if you put your factory information on this... thing... called a website, people all over the world will be able to see your products."

"On what? A website? Is it something like a shop?"

"Not at all. It's like... Imagine a shop that exists on a computer, and people can visit it from anywhere in the world."

"Young man, are you feeling well? How can a shop exist on a computer?"

Initial results were as challenging as anticipated. China Pages had to work hard to find customers who understood the value of an online presence. After a few years, Jack realized he was about five years ahead of the market. The infrastructure wasn't ready, the mindset wasn't ready, and the timing wasn't right.

But Jack learned from this "failure": **being right too early is the same as being wrong.** Timing isn't just important in business—it's everything. This lesson would later prove crucial when he launched Alibaba at just the right time.

A Government Turn

In 1998, Jack took a job with the Chinese government, heading a small technical unit in the Ministry of Foreign Trade and Economic Cooperation. For someone with an entrepreneurial spirit, this was like locking a lion in a cage.

But Jack used this time wisely. He studied how international trade worked, how small and medium-sized businesses struggled to connect with global markets, and how bureaucracy could help or hinder innovation.

Most importantly, he realized something profound: China was about to open up to the world in unprecedented ways. Small manufacturers and merchants were hungry for opportunities but had no way to reach international buyers. The internet could be a bridge, but it had to be built in the right way, at the right time, with the right approach.

After a year in government, Jack made a decision that shocked everyone who knew him: he was going to leave his stable, well-paying job and risk everything on the internet again.

His friends thought he was crazy. His family was worried. His wife... well, she had learned to trust Jack's crazy ideas.

The Birth of Alibaba: A Fairy Tale Begins

February 1999. Jack Ma's apartment in Hangzhou. Eighteen friends and colleagues filled his living room, sitting on whatever furniture was available, some on the floor. Jack stood before them, his eyes gleaming with excitement, about to pitch an idea that would change everything.

"Friends," he began, *"I want to start a company that will help connect small businesses in China with customers around the world. We'll call it Alibaba."*

Why Alibaba? Jack explained: *"Alibaba is about helping small people achieve big dreams. In the story, Alibaba says 'Open your door,' and a treasure trove opens. We're going to help small businesses say 'Open your door,' to global opportunities."*

The idea was revolutionary for its simplicity: creating an online marketplace where Chinese manufacturers could showcase their products to international buyers. No more expensive trade shows, no more middlemen who cut big slivers, no more barriers between manufacturer and buyer.

But what made this moment truly special: Jack asked everyone in the room to contribute whatever they could—not just money, but their dreams, their energy, their willingness to work 16 hours a day to create something extraordinary.

Some contributed a few thousand yuan. Others couldn't contribute money, but they offered their skills, their time, and their unwavering faith in Jack's vision. The total startup capital was $60,000—barely enough to rent an office and buy a computer.

Jack's promise to his team: *"If we succeed, we will all succeed together.*

> *"If we succeed, we will all succeed together. If we fail, we will all fail together. But we won't fail because we're going to work harder and dream bigger than anyone else."*

If we fail, we will all fail together. But we won't fail because we're going to work harder and dream bigger than anyone else."

That night, eighteen people decided to stake their futures on the crazy idea of a man who had been rejected from KFC.

Beautiful irony? These eighteen people would become the founding team of one of the world's most valuable companies. Their loyalty, creativity, and shared vision would prove more valuable than all the venture capital in Silicon Valley.

Early Struggles: Building a Rocket to Fly

Alibaba's first few months were extremely difficult. The team worked from Jack's cramped apartment, slept on air mattresses, ate instant noodles, debugged code at 3 a.m., and called potential customers who had no idea what the internet was, let alone why they might need a website.

The challenges were enormous:

- Most Chinese businesses didn't have computers
- Internet connections were slow and expensive
- International buyers were skeptical of Chinese quality
- The team was rapidly spending its small budget

But something magical was happening: the few businesses that connected with Alibaba were starting to see results. A small manufacturer in Guangzhou received an order from Germany. A textile company in Zhejiang connected with buyers in Brazil. The news began to spread.

During this time, Jack traveled constantly, visiting small factories and trading companies across China. He would sit down with owners, often in rural areas, and explain how the Internet could transform their businesses.

His pitch was always the same: *"You make great products, but the world doesn't know you exist. Let me introduce your products to customers in 200 countries. Let me help you transform a local business into a global one."*

The Investment That Changed Everything

By the end of 1999, Alibaba was gaining momentum but running out of money. Jack knew he needed serious investment to survive and grow. The problem? Most investors still didn't understand the Chinese internet market.

Then came Goldman Sachs and SoftBank.

These meetings became legendary. Jack, who still spoke imperfect English, stood before seasoned Wall Street investors and painted a picture of China's digital future with the passion of a true believer.

"Gentlemen," he would say, "you're not just investing in Alibaba. You're investing in the digitization of China. You're investing in connecting 1.4 billion people to the global economy."

Some investors were skeptical. The internet bubble in America was bursting. Many dot-com companies were failing. Why would Chinese e-commerce be any different?

Jack's answer was brilliant: "Because in the US, you're trying to move customers from physical stores to online stores. In China, most of our customers never even had access to a physical store. We're not competing with Walmart—we're building the first Walmart for millions of people."

The result? Goldman Sachs and SoftBank invested $25 million in Alibaba in 2000. But more than money, these partnerships gave Alibaba credibility and access to international expertise.

The eBay War: David vs. Goliath, Chinese Style

In 2003, eBay was the undisputed king of online marketplaces globally. When they entered China by purchasing EachNet, everyone assumed they would dominate the Chinese market just as they did everywhere else.

Everyone except Jack Ma:

Jack saw eBay's entry not as a threat, but as confirmation that the Chinese e-commerce market was about to explode. His answer? Launching Taobao—a consumer-to-consumer marketplace that would directly compete with the global giants.

The battle plan was bold:

- While eBay charged listing fees, Taobao would be completely free.
- While eBay used a Western-style auction format, Taobao would focus on fixed-price sales, which Chinese consumers preferred.

- While eBay limited contact between buyers and sellers, Taobao would encourage it through integrated chat features.

But here was the brilliant thing: Jack understood something about Chinese consumers that eBay missed. In a market lacking trust, buyers and sellers needed to talk, interact, and build relationships before a transaction.

eBay's answer? They continued to emphasize their global strategy, confident that their superior technology and brand recognition would prevail.

Jack's answer? "eBay is a shark in the sea, but I am a crocodile in the Yangtze River. In the river, the crocodile wins."

The Victory That Shook the World

What followed was one of the greatest David versus Goliath stories in business history. Within two years, Taobao had not only equaled eBay's market share in China—it had crushed it. By 2006, eBay had conceded defeat and left the Chinese market.

How did Jack Ma defeat one of the world's most successful internet companies?

1. He understood his customers better than competitors. Chinese consumers wanted to chat, negotiate, and build trust before buying. Taobao made this easy. eBay made it difficult.

2. He was willing to sacrifice short-term profits for long-term market share. While eBay focused on generating immediate revenue, Jack focused first on creating value for users, knowing that profits would come later.

3. He moved fast and adapted quickly. When users asked for features, Taobao implemented them within weeks. eBay's global bureaucracy took months.

4. He played to win, not to avoid losing. eBay was protecting a global business model. Jack was building a Chinese business from the ground up.

The lesson? Sometimes local knowledge and customer obsession trump global resources and superior technology. Sometimes the aggressive underdog wins by caring more, moving faster, and understanding the market better than the established player.

Expanding the Empire: More Than Just E-Commerce

With Taobao dominating Chinese consumer e-commerce, Jack began building what would become the Alibaba ecosystem. Each new business solved a real problem facing small businesses and consumers:

Alipay (2004): Chinese consumers didn't trust online payments. Jack created an escrow service that held buyers' payments until they confirmed they had received their products. This single innovation solved the trust problem that was holding back Chinese e-commerce.

Tmall (2008): As Chinese consumers became more sophisticated, they wanted branded products from established companies. Tmall became a platform for brands to reach Chinese consumers directly.

Alibaba Cloud (2009): As Chinese businesses went digital, they needed cloud computing services. Alibaba built the infrastructure that would power China's digital transformation.

Ant Financial (2014): Millions of Chinese lacked access to traditional banking. Ant Financial created digital financial services that brought banking to the masses.

Every business followed the same pattern: find a massive problem affecting millions of people. Build a solution that creates value for users first. Scale rapidly. Invest in profits thoughtfully.

The IPO That Broke Records

September 19, 2014. New York Stock Exchange. Jack Ma stood on a balcony overlooking the trading floor, watching Alibaba go public in the largest IPO in history at the time—$25 billion.

But what made this moment truly special: Jack wasn't just celebrating his own success. He was celebrating the success of the millions of small business owners who made their living on Alibaba's platform.

In his speech that day, Jack said: "Today, we're not just celebrating Alibaba going public. We're celebrating the dreams of every small business owner in China who dared to reach customers worldwide."

The figures were staggering:

- Alibaba was valued at $231 billion on its first day of trading.
- Jack's stake was worth $18 billion.
- Eighteen founders who started with him in their apartment suddenly became billionaires.
- But most importantly, millions of small businesses were empowered to reach global markets.

The Philosophy That Built an Empire

What made Jack Ma not just successful, but influential? His leadership philosophy offers profound lessons for anyone building anything meaningful:

1. Customers First, Employees Second, Shareholders Third. "If we make our customers successful, if we keep our employees happy, shareholders will naturally be happy. But if we focus on shareholders first, we will lose customers and employees."

2. Think Big, Start Small, Move Fast. "Don't try to solve all the world's problems at once. Pick one big problem, start with a simple solution, and improve it every day."

3. Embrace failure as a lesson "Before Alibaba, I failed three times in business. Each failure taught me something I couldn't have learned any other way. Your failures are your best teachers."

4. Technology should serve humanity, not replace it "We don't want to be a tech company that happens to be in business. We want to be a business company that happens to be using technology to solve human problems."

5. Success is about making others successful "The best businesses don't just make money—they make other people successful. Our job isn't to compete with small businesses—it's to help them compete globally."

> *"The best businesses don't just make money—they make other people successful.*

The Challenges of Success

Jack Ma's **inspiring journey** was fraught with difficulties despite achieving immense success. In 2020, Ant Financial's highly anticipated IPO was abruptly halted by Chinese regulators after Jack made public comments criticizing China's financial regulatory system.

This incident reminded everyone that even the most successful entrepreneurs face challenges that test their resilience and adaptability. Jack remained out of public life for several months, demonstrating his wisdom in knowing when to move forward and when to retreat.

The lesson? Success doesn't shield you from difficulties—it often creates new kinds of challenges. The same bold thinking that drives success can sometimes also create unexpected complications. True leadership means adapting your vision while remaining true to your core values.

The Global Impact of One Man's Vision

Let's discuss the scope of Jack Ma's impact on the world:

Economic Impact:

- Alibaba's platforms facilitate transactions worth over $1 trillion annually
- Millions of small businesses have been empowered to access global markets
- Countless jobs have been created across the Alibaba ecosystem
- Singles' Day has become the world's largest shopping event, generating over $74 billion in revenue in 2021

Social Impact:

- Rural communities in China gained access to markets previously unavailable to them
- Removed traditional barriers between manufacturers and consumers
- Digital payment systems brought financial services to underserved populations
- Cloud computing infrastructure accelerated digital transformation across Asia

Cultural Impact:

- Proved that Chinese companies can build global platforms
- Inspired a generation of entrepreneurs in developing countries
- Showed that customer-centric businesses can outperform technology-centric businesses
- Showed that local market knowledge can triumph over global resources.

Life Lessons from the Founder of Alibaba

Jack Ma's success story offers life lessons deeper than just business:

Lesson 1: Rejection is Redirection

Jack was rejected from 30 jobs, including KFC. If any of these companies had hired him, the world might never have known Alibaba. Sometimes what seems like a failure is actually luck saving you from the wrong opportunity and bringing you the right one.

Practical Application: Keep track of your rejections. Years later, you may realize they were the best things that happened to you.

Lesson 2: Timing Beats Technology

Jack wasn't the most technical founder, and Alibaba wasn't built on the most advanced technology. But Jack understood market timing and customer needs better than his competitors.

Practical Application: Don't wait for the perfect product or perfect skills. Focus on solving real problems for real people at the right time.

Lesson 3: Culture eats strategy for breakfast

Alibaba succeeded not just because they had the best strategy (although they had that too), but because they created a culture where people were willing to work incredibly hard toward a shared vision.

Practical Application: Whether you're building a business, leading a team, or working on a personal project, invest heavily in creating the right culture and mindset.

Lesson 4: Think Global, Act Local

Jack succeeded against global competitors by understanding local markets better than they did. He adapted global concepts to Chinese priorities and behaviors.

Practical Application: Don't just copy what works elsewhere. Understand your specific market, customers, and context, then adapt best practices accordingly.

Lesson 5: Success is a Team Sport

The eighteen people who started Alibaba with Jack weren't just employees—they were co-creators of a vision. Jack succeeded because he made others successful.

Practical Application: Your greatest successes will come from helping others achieve their dreams. Focus on creating value for others, and value will come back to you.

Current Chapter: Still Teaching, Still Learning

Today, Jack Ma continues to inspire through teaching and philanthropy. He has stepped back from day-to-day business operations to focus on education and rural development. His Jack Ma Foundation works to improve education in rural areas and support young entrepreneurs.

His current philosophy: "In my next life, I want to be a teacher again. Business is about making money, but teaching is about building people."

> *"In my next life, I want to be a teacher again. Business is about making money, but teaching is about building people."*

This evolution shows us something profound about true success: it's not about accumulating wealth or power -- it's about using your influence to bring positive change to the world.

Your Alibaba moment begins now

So, what does Jack Ma's incredibly inspiring journey mean to you?

Maybe you're sitting in your own metaphorical apartment, surrounded by friends and family who think your idea is crazy. Maybe you're collecting your own rejection letters, wondering if you'll ever find success. Maybe you feel too small to compete with established players in your field.

Jack's story teaches us this: Your current circumstances are not your final destination. Your rejections are not your reality. Your background doesn't determine your success.

The magic formula isn't complicated:

- Find a real problem that affects many people.
- Build a solution that puts customers first.
- Start small but think big.

- Persevere despite rejection and failure.
- Build a team that shares your vision.
- Adapt quickly when the market provides feedback.
- Never stop learning and growing.

Jack Ma started with $60,000 and eighteen friends. Today, Alibaba serves more than 1 billion customers worldwide. The gap between where you are and where you want to go isn't as wide as you think -- it's simply filled with work that most people aren't willing to do.

From failure to success isn't just a catchphrase – it's a predictable process when you have the right mindset and take consistent action.

Interactive Challenge: Build Your Own Empire

Ready to apply Jack Ma's principles to your own inspiring journey? Here are practical challenges to help you think like a global achiever:

Week 1: Problem-Finding Mission

Like Jack, who identified the gap between Chinese manufacturers and global buyers:

- **Daily Practice:** Spend 30 minutes a day looking for problems people complain about.
- **Research Challenge:** Ask 10 people about their biggest pain points at work or in life.
- **Documentation:** Keep a "problem diary" -- you're looking for problems that affect many people but don't have a good solution.

Week 2: Rejection Collection

Like Jack, who embraced rejection with 30 job applications:

- **Application Challenge:** Apply for something you want but think you might not get.
- **Pitch Practice:** Present an idea to 5 people and get feedback (even if they say no).
- **Reframe Exercise:** Write about a past rejection and identify what it taught you or how it nudged you toward something better.

Week 3: Customer-First Experiment

Embrace Jack's passion for customer value:

- **Value Creation:** Do something valuable for someone without expecting anything in return
- **Feedback Loop:** Ask three potential customers what they want that doesn't yet exist
- **Solution Design:** Create a simple solution to a problem you've identified (even if it is just a detailed plan)

Week 4: Team Building Challenge

Remember, Jack succeeded with 18 friends, not alone:

- **Network Expansion:** Connect with three people who share your interests or goals
- **Skill Sharing:** Teach someone something you know well
- **Collaboration:** Work on a small project with someone, even if it's just for learning

Reflection Questions:

- What problem do you see that others ignore or assume is "just the way it is"?

- If you could help 1 million people with one solution, what would that solution be?
- What rejection in your life might actually be keeping you from the wrong path?
- If you had 18 friends willing to stake their future on your vision, what vision would be worth that level of commitment?
- If you knew that perseverance and customer focus could overcome any initial setbacks, what would you try?

The Wisdom of a Fortune Cookie

Jack Ma often says: *"Today is hard, tomorrow will be worse, but the day after tomorrow will be beautiful."*

> *"Today is hard, tomorrow will be worse, but the day after tomorrow will be beautiful."*

This isn't just inspirational sayings -- it's a fundamental truth about the reality of success. The hardest moment often comes just before success. The darkest hour is just before dawn. The final rejection often comes just before the acceptance that changes everything.

Your **"day after tomorrow"** is waiting for you. But it's not waiting passively -- it's waiting for you to go through today's hardship and tomorrow's misery with unwavering faith in your vision.

Jack Ma was rejected from KFC. Today, Alibaba's annual revenue exceeds the entire market value of KFC's parent company.

The question isn't whether you'll face rejection, failure, and doubt. You will.

The question is whether you'll turn those experiences into stepping stones or let them become obstacles.

Jack chose the stepping stone. He turned every "no" into fuel for a big "yes." He turned every closed door into inspiration to open your own.

Your empire is waiting to be built. Your Alibaba moment is closer than you think. Your "Open it up" isn't magic words – it's consistent action combined with unwavering faith in your ability to create value for others.

The treasure trove of your dreams is real. But like Alibaba's cave, it opens only to those courageous enough to keep trying even when everyone else has given up.

Your adventure begins now. Make it legendary.

"The most important thing you should have is patience. You should learn from your competitor, but never copy. If you copy, you die." - Jack Ma

The most important thing you should have is patience. You should learn from your competitor, but never copy. If you copy, you die."

Choose perseverance. Choose innovation. Choose to start your empire today.

Chapter 4

Walt Disney (USA) – From Denial to Magical Empire

Photo: Unknown author / Public Domain / Wikimedia Commons – https://commons.wikimedia.org/wiki/File:Walt-Disney-1956.jpg, retrieved on Nov. 12, 2025

The Inspiring Journey of a Man Who Turned Dreams into Reality

The Question That Changes Everything

What if I told you that the man who created the most magical place on Earth was once fired for "lack of imagination"? What if the man who brought smiles to the faces of millions of children around the world was told he had no creative talent? Would you believe that the founder ofa $187 billion company started with just $40 and a suitcase full of failures?

This is no fairy tale—even if it seems that way. This is the true success story of Walt Disney, a man whose journey from failure to success proves that sometimes our biggest failures are actually the setting for our most incredible comebacks.

Right now, as you read these words, somewhere in the world, a child is laughing at Mickey Mouse's pranks, a family is creating magical memories at Disneyland, and dreamers are finding inspiration in the stories born from the mind of a man who refused to let denial dictate his destiny.

But Walt Disney's path to becoming a global achiever wasn't paved with fairy dust—it was built on resilience, watered with tears, and illuminated by an unwavering belief in the impossible.

Are you ready to learn how one man's refusal to give up changed the world forever? Let's dive into this inspiring journey that will show you how to turn setbacks into comebacks.

The Boy Who Dared to Dream Big

Imagine the picture, the year is 1908, and a seven-year-old boy sits in front of his house in Marceline, Missouri, sketching everything he sees. The passion gripping the pencil in his tiny hands seems incredibly intense for someone his age. This isn't just any child playing—this is Walt Disney, searching for his life's purpose before he even knew what it meant.

But Walt's childhood wasn't filled with the magic we associate with his name today. Born on December 5, 1901, in Chicago, Illinois, Walt's dreams often took a backseat to harsh realities. His father, Elias Disney, was a strict man who believed in discipline above all else. The family struggled financially, and when Walt was just ten years old, they moved from Chicago to a farm in Missouri.

Can you imagine waking up at 4:30 every morning at such a young age to deliver newspapers before school? That was Walt's reality. While other children played, Walt worked. While others slept soundly, Walt trudged through the snow and rain, carrying newspapers that seemed heavier than he was. His father was strict, often harsh, believing that hard work—not creativity—was the key to survival.

But that's why Walt's story is so powerful: instead of letting these challenges crush his spirit, he found magic in the ordinary. On those morning newspaper trips, Walt watched the sunlight dance on the snow. He watched the movements of animals, the play of shadows on buildings. Every experience became material for his growing imagination.

His mother, Flora, was his refuge. She encouraged his drawing, understanding that her son possessed something special—something that couldn't be measured in dollars or defined by conventional success. When Walt sold his first sketches to neighbors at the age of seven, earning his first money, Flora saw that this wasn't just a kid making pocket money, but a future visionary taking his first steps.

This is your first life lesson from Walt Disney: **Your circumstances don't determine your destiny—your reaction to them does.** Walt could have been filled with bitterness about his difficult childhood. Instead, he decided to see the wonder in everyday moments, and this decision would later inspire wonder for millions.

The Crushing Burden of "You're Not Good Enough"

Let's fast forward to the early 1920s. Walt Disney, now a young man with big dreams and even bigger ambitions, walks into the Kansas City Star newspaper office. He's applied for a cartoonist job, his portfolio tucked under his arm like a treasure trove of possibilities. As he spread his drawings on the editor's desk, waiting for validation, for recognition, for someone to say, "Yes, we believe in you," his heart was probably pounding.

Instead, he heard words that will haunt many people for the rest of their lives: *"You lack imagination and you have no good ideas."*

> *"You lack imagination and you have no good ideas."*

Let's consider this for a moment. Walt Disney—the man who would later create Mickey Mouse, revolutionize animation, and build theme parks that spark the imagination of millions—was told he lacked imagination. The man whose *"good ideas"* would generate billions of dollars and create a global entertainment empire—was told he had no good ideas.

How would you have responded? Would you have crushed your dreams along with your drawings? Would you have accepted that harsh judgment as the final word on your potential?

Walt felt the sting of rejection deep within his soul. Years later, he would admit that being fired from the Kansas City Star was one of the most painful experiences of his young life. But here, Walt's story becomes a masterclass in resilience: he refused to let someone else's opinion dictate his reality.

Instead of giving up, Walt turned his disappointment into determination. He started his own business, founding Laugh-O-Gram Films in 1922. Finally, he thought, he could create cartoons of his own imagination, tell the stories burning within him, and prove those critics wrong.

For a brief, shining moment, it seemed Walt's perseverance was paying off. Laugh-O-Gram Films produced numerous animated shorts, and Walt poured every ounce of his creativity and energy into making them successful. He would work eighteen-hour days, subsisting on beans and bread, and believing with every fiber of his being that his dreams were finally coming true.

Then came 1923 – the year that should have broken Walt Disney forever.Laugh-O-Gram Films went bankrupt. Completely, utterly bankrupt. Walt's first real venture in the entertainment industry had failed terribly. He was 22 years old, broke, and facing the harsh reality that perhaps those who doubted him were right.

Look at Walt at that moment of devastating failure. All his savings gone. His business dreams shattered. His employees gone. Standing in an empty office that once buzzed with creative energy, now silent except for the sound of his heartbeat and the weight of crushing disappointment.

This is where most people's stories would end. This is where most people would pack up their dreams, accept a *"sensible"* job, and spend the rest of their lives wishing they had. But Walt Disney wasn't like most people.

Life lesson: Failure isn't the opposite of success—it's its foundation. Every great achiever has a moment when everything seems to fall apart, when the world says *"give up,"* but something deep inside whispers *"keep going."* Walt was about to discover that his biggest failures were actually his greatest teachers.

The $40 Miracle: When the Bottomless Foothills Become Your Launchpad

Have you ever had so little that your entire fortune could fit in your pocket? Walt Disney did. In 1923, with Laugh-O-Gram Films bankrupt and his dreams in ruins, Walt made a decision that would change entertainment history forever. With just $40 to his name—about $600 today—he bought a one-way train ticket to Hollywood.

Imagine that train journey. A young man with nothing but $40, a cardboard suitcase tied with a string, and an unshakable belief that somehow, some way, he would succeed in the film capital. No connections, no guarantees, no safety net. Just pure, audacious faith in himself and his dreams.

When Walt arrived in Hollywood, he had no place to live, no job waiting for him, or even a clear plan. What he did possess was far more powerful: the absolute determination that his failures had prepared him for something better. He had learned painful but invaluable lessons about business, creativity, and the resilience needed to turn dreams into reality.

Walt's first priority wasn't finding a lucrative job in the film industry—but rather survival. He moved in with his brother Roy, who was recovering from tuberculosis in a California hospital. Together, they scraped together enough money to set up a small animation studio in their uncle's garage. The Disney Brothers Studio was born—not in a shiny office building, but in a cramped garage where two brothers refused to give up on their dreams.

Those early days tested every ounce of Walt's resolve. He and Roy worked around the clock, creating animation by hand—a painfully slow and incredibly demanding process. Walt would create hundreds of individual images, each slightly different from the last, to create just a few seconds of animated motion. His fingers ached, his eyes strained, and his back ached from hunched over the drawing board for sixteen hours.

But something magical was happening in that small garage. Walt was developing his art, refining his vision, and laying the foundation for what would become the Disney empire. Every rejected idea, every financial struggle, every moment of doubt was molding him into the visionary the world needed.

Breakthrough came when Walt created a character that would change everything: Oswald the Lucky Rabbit. The character was a hit, brought a steady income, and finally gave Walt hope that he could make a living doing what he loved. Success seemed within arm's reach.

Then came another devastating blow that would have destroyed a less resilient man.

In 1928, Walt discovered that his distributor had betrayed him. Not only had they stolen the rights to Oswald the Lucky Rabbit, but they had also lured away most of his animation staff with higher salaries. In one crushing moment, Walt lost his character, his team, and everything he had worked so hard to build.

Imagine Walt sitting on the train returning from that disastrous business meeting in New York, his wife Lillian beside him, facing another catastrophic failure. Most people would have been devastated by this betrayal, this theft of their life's work.

But Walt Disney did something extraordinary. As the train carried him back to California, instead of sinking into defeat, he began sketching. And from his pencil emerged a new character—a cheerful, optimistic mouse with big, round ears and an even bigger personality.

He called him Mickey Mouse.

Life lesson: Your greatest comebacks often come from your most painful losses. When life takes something from you, it might be making room for something even better. Walt's loss of Oswald led directly to the creation of Mickey Mouse—and Mickey Mouse paved the way for everything else.

The Birth of Magic: When Dreams Take Shape

"It all started with a mouse." These five simple words became one of the most famous sentences in entertainment history, but they barely hint at the incredible journey that brought Mickey Mouse tolife.

"It all started with a mouse."

After losing Oswald, Walt threw himself obsessively into developing this new character. He understood that Mickey Mouse wasn't just another cartoon character—he was Walt's chance to prove that creativity, originality, and pure perseverance could overcome betrayal and failure.

Working in his small studio, Walt and his small team of loyal animators began creating Mickey's debut film: "Steamboat Willie." But Walt had an idea that was considered revolutionary, even crazy, at the time. He wanted to synchronize sound with animation—something that had never been successfully done before.

Everyone told him it was impossible. The technology was too new, too unreliable. The costs would be enormous. Audiences wouldn't care for a talking cartoon mouse. But Walt had learned something important from all his previous failures: the biggest risks often lead to the greatest rewards.

He put everything—and I mean everything—into perfecting "Steamboat Willie." He mortgaged his house, borrowed money from anyone who would lend him money, and worked eighteen-hour days to ensure every detail was perfect. Walt himself provided Mickey's voice, a squeaky, optimistic voice that matched the character's indomitable personality.

The premiere of "Steamboat Willie" on November 18, 1928, was a moment that changed entertainment forever. When audiences saw Mickey Mouse whistling and dancing in perfect synchronization with the music, something magical happened. They didn't just see a cartoon—they fell in love with a character who embodied the same optimism and resilience that had carried Walt through his darkest moments.

The response was explosive. Suddenly, everyone wanted to see more Mickey Mouse cartoons. Walt had not only survived his latest setback—he had revolutionized the entire industry.

But Walt's vision extended far beyond a single character or even a series of cartoons. As Mickey Mouse's popularity grew, Walt began to dream bigger. He envisioned longer films, richer stories, and innovations that would push the boundaries of animation.

His next impossible dream? A full-length animated film.

Once again, everyone told him he was crazy. In the 1930s, animation was for short films shown before the main feature. No one would watch an entire film of cartoons, critics said. It would be financial suicide.

Walt listened to these objections, smiled, and kept working.

For four years, Walt and his growing team poured their hearts into making *"Snow White and the Seven Dwarfs."* The project nearly bankrupted the studio several times. Walt had to show unfinished scenes to potential investors, providing all the character voices himself and acting out the story with such passion that the grown men believed in magic.

For four years, Walt and his growing team poured their hearts into making *"Snow White and the Seven Dwarfs."*

The film's budget ballooned from an estimated $250,000 to over $1.4 million—an astronomical sum for any film of the 1930s, let alone an animated film. As costs escalated and deadlines approached, many within the studio began calling the project "Disney's Folly."

Walt never wavered. He had learned to trust his vision completely,especially when—that vision seemed impossible to others.

On December 21, 1937, "Snow White and the Seven Dwarfs" premiered before a stunned audience. As the final scene played and the credits rolled, the theater erupted in the longest standing ovation in film history. Critics who had predicted disaster declared it a masterpiece. The film grossed over $8 million worldwide—making it one of the most successful films of its time.

Walt Disney had just proven that there's no such thing as the impossible—there are only things that haven't been done yet.

Life lesson: When everyone says your dream is impossible, you're probably on your way to something extraordinary. The greater the doubt from others, the greater the potential for success.

Building an Empire: Making the Impossible Real

By the 1950s, Walt Disney had already achieved what most people would consider the success of many lifetimes. He had created beloved characters, revolutionized animation, and built a thriving entertainment company. At 50, he could easily have settled into a comfortable retirement, content with his extraordinary achievements.

Instead, Walt announced his most ambitious dream: he wanted to build a theme park like nothing the world had ever seen.

The idea came to him during trips to amusement parks with his daughters. Walt watched his children having fun on simple rides and attractions, but he envisioned something far more magical—a place where families could step into the stories and characters he created, where imagination became reality, where adults could remember what it felt like to believe in magic.

He called it Disneyland.

Once again, everyone thought Walt had lost his mind. In the 1950s, amusement parks were cheap, run-down places that were more reminiscent of carnivals than family entertainment. The idea of spending millions of dollars to build an elaborate theme park seemed the ultimate folly.

Banks refused to give him a loan. His own brother, Roy, who was usually supportive, expressed serious doubts. Entertainment industry experts declared the concept economically impossible. "Who would come to Anaheim to see a theme park?" they laughed.

"Who would come to Anaheim to see a theme park?"

Walt listened to all the objections, then did what he always does: he found a way to make his vision a reality.

He sold his vacation home, took out a loan against his life insurance, and even sold his beloved train collection. When traditional financing still wasn't enough, Walt did something unprecedented—he partnered with the new medium of television, creating "The Mickey Mouse Club" and "Walt Disney Disneyland" to help finance his dream park.

The construction of Disneyland was a masterclass in turning obstacles into opportunities. Every problem became a puzzle to be solved, every disadvantage an opportunity for innovation. When landscaping costs threatened to devastate the budget, Walt's team devised new techniques to create a green environment in a cost-effective manner. When ride technology didn't exist, they invented that too. Walt was personally involved in every detail, from the height of the castle's turrets to the flavor of the ice cream sold on Main Street. He understood that Disneyland wasn't just a business venture—it was the physical manifestation of all his beliefs about the power of imagination to create joy.

On July 17, 1955, a week before Disneyland was scheduled to open, disaster struck. The park wasn't even close to being ready. The freshly laid asphalt hadn't set properly in the California heat, causing women's high heels to sink into the ground. Plumbing problems meant that some areas had either working restrooms or working water fountains, but not both. Attractions repeatedly broke down during testing.

The press, already skeptical about Walt's ambitious project, began writing elegy for Disneyland even before it opened. "Walt Disney's $17 Million Nightmare," read one headline.

Opening day itself was chaos. Invitations to invited guests were forged, leading to massive crowds. The Mark Twain Riverboat nearly sank from overloading. Restaurants ran out of food. Many attractions simply didn't work.

Most people viewed opening day as confirmation that the critics were right, that Disneyland was indeed "Disney's Folly." Walt saw it differently. Years later, he would say, "Disneyland is a labor of love. Anyone can see that. When we opened Disneyland, I knew we had a success on our hands."

> *"Disneyland is a labor of love. Anyone can see that. When we opened Disneyland, I knew we had a success on our hands."*

He was right. Within months, Disneyland had transformed from a chaotic opening day disaster into America's most popular tourist destination. Families traveled hundreds of miles to experience Walt's vision. The park, which critics had said would never work, was soon hosting millions of visitors each year.

But Walt's vision for Disneyland went beyond commercial success. He had created something that touched people's souls—a place where parents and children could share wonder together, where imagination was celebrated, where the magic of storytelling became a tactile experience.

As Walt walked around his completed park, watching families create magical memories together, he reflected on the incredible journey that had brought him to this moment. From the boy who was told he lacked imagination to the man who created the most imaginative place on Earth—it was a transformation that proved the power of never giving up on your dreams.

Life lesson: Your biggest dreams require the biggest risks. If your goal doesn't scare you at least a little, it's probably not big enough to change your life or the world.

Wisdom of a Dreamer: Life Lessons That Change Lives

Walt Disney's journey from negativity to global success gives us a deep understanding of what it takes to turn dreams into reality. His words, born from decades of struggle and triumph, continue to inspire millions around the world.

"We keep moving forward, opening new doors, and doing new things because we are curious... and curiosity keeps leading us down new paths." This quote encapsulates Walt's fundamental approach to life and success. He understood that stagnation is the enemy of achievement, that constant growth and exploration are essential for anyone who wants to make a lasting impact.

> *"We keep moving forward, opening new doors, and doing new things because we are curious... and curiosity keeps leading us down new paths."*

Reflect on your own life for a moment. When was the last time you opened a new door? When was the last time you let curiosity lead you down an unknown path? Walt's success came not from playing it safe, but from constantly pushing beyond your comfort zone, never settling for "good enough."

Walt also understood the power of resilience in the face of adversity. *"All the adversities in my life, all my troubles and obstacles, have made me stronger,"* he once said. This isn't just positive thinking—it's a fundamental truth about how extraordinary people are made.

> *"All the adversities in my life, all my troubles and obstacles, have made me stronger,"*

Every rejection Walt faced taught him something valuable. Being fired from the Kansas City Star taught him that other people's opinions don't define his potential. The bankruptcy of Laugh-O-Gram Films taught him important lessons about business management. The theft of Oswald the Lucky Rabbit taught him to protect his intellectual property and trust his creative instincts.

Without these setbacks, Walt Disney wouldn't have become Walt Disney. His failures weren't distractions from the path to success—they were the path itself.

Most importantly, Walt understood that dreams without action remain mere fantasies. *"The way to get started is to quit talking and start doing,"* he advised. In our modern world of social media and instant gratification, it's easy to get caught up in the excitement of possibility, talking about your dreams and sharing your plans, and never taking concrete action.

> *"The way to get started is to quit talking and start doing,"*

Walt was different. He transformed dreams into detailed plans, plans into specific actions, and actions into extraordinary realities. When he conceived Mickey Mouse, he didn't just sketch the character—he produced films, developed merchandising, and built an entire entertainment empire around that vision.

His approach to teamwork was equally revolutionary. *"You can design and create, and build the most wonderful places in the world. But it takes people to make a dream a reality,"* Walt observed. He understood that no one achieves greatness alone; that

"You can design and create, and build the most wonderful places in the world. But it takes people to make a dream a reality,"

success requires the ability to inspire others to share his vision and work toward common goals.

Walt's leadership style was unique for his time. He didn't just give orders—he shared his vision so compellingly that people wanted to be a part of making it a reality. He created an environment where creativity flourished, where people felt empowered to contribute their best ideas, where innovation was only encouraged.

This lesson is crucial for anyone seeking significant success in any field. Your dreams may start with you, but they will only become reality when you learn to inspire others to join you in pursuing them.

Life Lesson: Success is not a solo journey. The world's most successful people are those who can transform their personal vision into a shared mission that others are excited to support.

From Struggle to Power: The Transformation Process

Walt Disney's transformation from a struggling cartoonist to a global icon didn't happen overnight. It was a gradual process of growth, learning, and constant rebuilding that offers valuable insights for anyone facing similar challenges.

In his early twenties, Walt was reactive—responding to setbacks with frustration and uncertainty. When he was fired from the Kansas City Star, he felt defeated. When Laugh-O-Gram Films failed, he questioned whether he had what it took to succeed in entertainment.

But every failure taught him something important about resilience. By the time he lost Oswald the Lucky Rabbit, Walt had developed a different response to failure. Instead of wallowing in defeat, he channeled his disappointment into creative energy, using the long train journey home to develop Mickey Mouse.

This shift from reactive to proactive thinking is one of the most important changes anyone can make. Reactive people let circumstances dictate their emotions and actions. Proactive people use circumstances as raw material to create better outcomes.

Walt also learned to see patterns where others saw only chaos. When "Snow White and the Seven Dwarfs" faced budget overruns and production delays, Walt didn't panic. He had learned from previous projects that extraordinary work requires extraordinary commitment. He trusted the process, knowing that success often seems impossible until it becomes inevitable.

This pattern recognition allowed Walt to take calculated risks that others might have considered reckless. When he decided to build Disneyland, he wasn't taking a blind gamble. He was applying lessons learned from decades of turning impossible dreams into profitable realities.

Most importantly, Walt learned to view failure as feedback rather than judgment. Early in his career, when the Kansas City Star fired him for a lack of imagination, Walt internalized that criticism as a judgment about his fundamental abilities. Later in life, when critics said Disneyland would never work, Walt heard the criticism as valuable information about market expectations—information he could use to make his vision even more compelling.

This shift in perspective is transformative. When you stop viewing criticism and failures as judgments about your worth or ability, you begin to see them as data points that can help refine your approach and improve results.

Walt's emotional intelligence also developed dramatically over time. The young man who was devastated by early rejections became someone who could maintain optimism and clarity even in the face of overwhelming challenges. He learned to separate his emotions from his decision-making, allowing him to think strategically even during difficult moments.

This emotional mastery wasn't about suppressing emotions—Walt remained passionate and enthusiastic throughout his life. Rather, it was about channeling emotions productively, using passion as fuel for perseverance rather than allowing discouragement to derail progress.

Life Lesson: Personal transformation is the foundation of external success. Before Walt Disney could transform the entertainment industry, he had to transform himself—his way of thinking, his response to failure, his ability to inspire others, and his ability to persevere through impossible challenges.

The Ripple Effect: How One Man's Dreams Change the World

The true measure of Walt Disney's success isn't found in box office receipts or theme park attendance figures—though those numbers are staggering. The real impact of Walt's journey lies in how his refusal to accept limitations created possibilities for millions of others.

Today, The Walt Disney Company employs more than 220,000 people worldwide. Each of these jobs exists because one person refused to let rejection define their destiny. Behind every employment figure is a family nurtured, dreams pursued, creative talents cultivated, and lives enriched by being part of something bigger than themselves.

But the ripple effects extend far beyond direct employment. Innovations in Disney's animation technology revolutionized filmmaking, inspiring countless other creators to push the boundaries of what's possible. Techniques developed for Disney films became industry standards, helping other studios tell more compelling visual stories.

The concept of immersive entertainment, which Walt pioneered with Disneyland, has influenced everything from museum design to retail environments to corporate training programs. Walt's insight that people crave experiences that engage their imagination has shaped our thinking about entertainment, education, and even architecture.

Consider the countless children who have been inspired by Disney films to pursue careers in animation, filmmaking, music, or other creative fields. Consider the families who have bonded over shared Disney experiences. Consider the dreamers who have found courage in Disney stories about ordinary characters achieving extraordinary things.

Walt's influence also extends to business philosophy. His approach to customer experience—an obsessive focus on creating magical moments rather than simply selling products—has been studied and adopted by companies in every industry. The idea that business success comes from exceeding customer expectations, rather than meeting them, can be traced directly to Walt's vision for Disneyland.

This is the final lesson from Walt Disney's inspiring journey: When you refuse to give up on your dreams, you don't just change your own life—you create possibilities for others that wouldn't otherwise exist.

Every person who has ever been inspired by a Disney film, every child who has experienced wonder at a Disney park, every creative professional who has been influenced by Disney's innovations—they all share the legacy of a man who refused to admit that he or she "lacked imagination."

Life lesson: Your dreams aren't just important to you, but to everyone whose life your creation will touch. When you give up on your vision, you're not just limiting yourself—you're depriving the world of the unique contribution that only you can make.

Numbers Tell the Story: Measuring the Achievement of Dreams

Sometimes inspiration needs to be backed by hard facts, and Walt Disney's success story provides some truly startling numbers that show how far perseverance and vision can take you.

Remember, Walt Disney began his Hollywood journey with $40 in his pocket. Today, The Walt Disney Company has a market value of over $187 billion. To put this in perspective, Walt turned his initial $40 investment into a company worth more than the GDP of most countries. This represents a return on investment that defies conventional financial wisdom and proves that the greatest returns come from betting on seemingly impossible dreams.

Walt's personal achievements are equally impressive. He won 22 Academy Awards in his lifetime—the most by any individual in history. These weren't just technical awards, but recognitions of breakthroughs in storytelling, animation, and entertainment innovation. Each award represented years of work, countless late nights, and the kind of perfectionist focus that separates the good from the exceptional.

The reach of Walt's creations is mind-boggling. Mickey Mouse is recognized by 98% of children worldwide—making him more recognizable than most world leaders. Disney films have been translated into dozens of languages and entertained billions of people on every continent. "Snow White and the Seven Dwarfs" alone has been seen by an estimated 200 million people since its release in 1937.

Disneyland revolutionized the concept of theme parks. When it opened in 1955, there was no destination comparable to it anywhere in the world. Today, Disney theme parks host more than 150 million visitors annually—roughly equal to the population of Russia. These aren't just tourists taking a quick look; they're families investing significant time and money to experience Walt's vision of magical entertainment.

Disneyland revolutionized the concept of theme parks. When it opened in 1955, there was no destination comparable to it anywhere in the world. Today, Disney theme parks host more than 150 million visitors annually—roughly equal to the population of

Russia. These aren't just tourists taking a quick look; these are families investing significant time and money to experience Walt's vision of magical entertainment.

The economic impact extends far beyond Disney's direct operations. Studies show that Disney World alone generates more than $75 billion annually for the Florida economy, supporting more than 460,000 jobs across the state. Similar economic impacts exist around every Disney property around the world.

But perhaps the most impressive numbers relate to Walt's impact on the entire entertainment industry. Before Walt, animated films were short novelties shown before the main feature. Today, animated films regularly gross more than $1 billion worldwide and are considered major cultural phenomena. The global animation industry, which essentially did not exist before Walt's innovations, now generates over $270 billion annually.

These numbers aren't just statistics—they represent the tangible impact of refusing to accept limits. They prove that when someone with vision persists through failure and rejection, ultimate success can surpass even the most optimistic projections.

Life lesson: Don't let the modesty of your current resources limit the magnitude of your dreams. Walt's journey from $40 to $187 billion proves that the size of your starting point has no bearing on the size of your potential end points.

Your Magic Kingdom Awaits: Acting on Your Dreams

As we reach the end of Walt Disney's incredible story, the most important question isn't what he achieved—but what his journey means for your life and dreams.

Right now, you might be facing a rejection letter from your Kansas City Star. Perhaps you're dealing with a failed business venture, a creative project that didn't find an audience, or a dream that seems impossible to achieve. Maybe you're sitting on your metaphorical train with just $40 in your pocket, wondering if you have the strength to start over.

Walt Disney's story gives you proof that your current circumstances don't determine your ultimate fate. But proof isn't enough—you need a plan to apply these lessons to your journey.

First, embrace failure as a lesson. Every loss Walt faced taught him something essential about business, creativity, leadership, or perseverance. Your failures aren't proof that you should quit—they're the tuition fee for your ultimate success. Start viewing every disappointment as valuable data that brings you closer to success.

Second, develop unwavering vision. Walt succeeded because he could see possibilities that others missed. When others saw only a failed business venture, he could imagine Mickey Mouse. When others saw only empty orange groves, he could envision Disneyland. Your ability to see beyond current limitations is your most powerful asset. Spend time every day visualizing your goals as already achieved, experiencing feelings of success, and planning specific steps to make your vision a reality.

Third, systematically build your resilience. Walt's ability to recover from setbacks wasn't a natural talent—it was a skill he developed through practice. Start building your resilience by taking small risks, learning from small failures, and gradually increasing your ability to handle bigger challenges. Resilience is like a muscle—the more you exercise it, the stronger it becomes.

Fourth, find ways to turn obstacles into opportunities. When Walt lost Oswald the Lucky Rabbit, he created Mickey Mouse. When traditional financing wasn't available for Disneyland, he pioneered television partnerships. Your biggest challenges often contain the seeds of your greatest successes. Ask yourself: "How can I use this problem to create something even better?"

> Ask yourself: *"How can I use this problem to create something even better?"*

Fifth, never underestimate the power of consistent action. Walt didn't achieve success with one brilliant idea—he achieved success with thousands of small actions, consistently performed over decades. Identify daily habits that will move you toward your goals, then practice those habits with the same dedication Walt displayed when drawing hundreds of animation frames by hand.

Your task for this week:

Pick a dream you've been putting off because it seems too difficult or impractical. Spend 30 minutes writing a detailed plan for the first three steps toward making that dream a reality. Don't worry about having all the answers—even Walt didn't have them when he bought that $40 train ticket to Hollywood. Focus on forward momentum, not perfect planning.

Remember: Walt Disney was once a struggling young man who had more rejection letters than job offers, more failures than successes, and more reasons to quit than to continue. The difference between Walt Disney and thousands of other talented people who gave up their dreams wasn't natural ability—it was a refusal to let circumstances define their future.

Your magical kingdom is waiting for you to build it. Your Mickey Mouse is waiting for you to create it. Your success is waiting for you to persist long enough to find it.

Only one question remains: will you?

Interactive Element: Your Personal Disney Challenge

Reflection Questions:

- What "Kansas City Star" rejection have you experienced in your life? How did you respond then, and how might you respond differently now?
- If you could start somewhere new with only $40 and your biggest dream, which dream would you choose?
- What is your Mickey Mouse equivalent—a simple idea that can transform into something extraordinary if you give it your full attention?
- Which of Walt's quotes resonates most powerfully with your current situation, and why?
- What would your personal "Disneyland" look like—a tangible manifestation of your dreams that others could experience?

Action Challenges:

Week 1: Vision Challenge Write a detailed description of your life five years from now if all your current dreams came true. Include specific details about what you would be doing, how you would be feeling, and what impact you would be having on others.

Week 2: Perseverance Challenge Identify a skill that's essential to your dreams but that you've been putting off because it's difficult. Promise to practice that skill for 30 minutes a day for the next month.

Week 3: Innovation Challenge Find a problem in your field or industry that everyone believes is "just the way it is." Spend a week brainstorming creative solutions, no matter how impossible they seem.

Week 4: Legacy Challenge Define the specific positive impact you want your life's work to have on others. Write a paragraph describing how the world will be different because you refused to give up on your dreams.

Remember Walt's words: *"Doing the impossible is fun."* Your impossible dream is waiting for you to make it fun, real, and your own.

"Doing the impossible is fun."

The magical kingdom of your potential is ready to be created. The only question is: when will you break ground?

"All our dreams can come true, if we have the courage to pursue them." - Walt Disney

Your adventure begins now. Your dreams are calling you. Answer them.

> *"All our dreams can come true, if we have the courage to pursue them."*

Closing: Your Journey Begins Here

As we conclude this extraordinary journey of Walt Disney, I want to share one final thing with you. This story isn't just a biography of one person—it's a map of your own possibilities.

Every great achievement begins with a simple decision: the decision not to give up. Walt made that decision the day he was fired from the Kansas City Star. He made that decision again when Laugh-O-Gram Films went bankrupt. He made that decision again and again, with every obstacle, with every loss, every moment when it would have been easier to give up.

And now it's your turn.

Whatever challenge you face—whether it's financial hardship, creative block, or simply the fear that your dream is too big—remember that Walt Disney has been there too. He felt the same fears, faced the same doubts, and spent the same nights when success seemed impossible.

But he never gave up. And neither should you.

Starting today, every morning when you wake up, ask yourself: "How can I take one step towards my dream today?" It could be a small step—one sketch, one phone call, ten minutes to learn a new skill. But every small step brings you closer to that magical moment when your "impossible" dream suddenly becomes an inevitable reality.

> *"How can I take one step towards my dream today?"*

The world is waiting for your unique contribution. Your Mickey Mouse, your Disneyland, your magical kingdom—they're all waiting for you to bring them to life.

So, get up. Dream. Get started. Your impossible journey begins right now.

"All dreams begin with a wish. And all wishes begin with courage. "Your courage, your time, your journey—right now.

> *"All dreams begin with a wish. And all wishes begin with courage."*

Chapter 5

J.K. Rowling (UK) – The Magic of Never Giving Up

Photo Credit: Daniel Ogren, *J. K. Rowling reads excerpts fromHarry Potter and the Philosopher's Stoneduring the Easter Egg Roll at the White House* (2010). Licensed under CC-BY-2.0. Source: Wikimedia Commons — https://commons.wikimedia.org/wiki/File:J._K._Rowling_2010.jpg

What if I told you that one of the world's most beloved authors was once so poor she couldn't even afford to heat her apartment?

Imagine the scene: a single mother, hunched over a table in a small Edinburgh café, writing furiously in her notebook, while her young daughter sleeps in a stroller beside her. She's dressed in layers because she can't afford heating. Rejection letters pile up on her desk like autumn leaves. Publishers laugh at her "unrealistic" fantasy about a young wizard. She's living on welfare and often wonders if she's fooling herself about her talent.

This same woman would go on to create the most successful book series in history, become the first billionaire author, and inspire millions around the world. Her name? Joanne Kathleen Rowling – though the world knows her simply as J.K. Rowling.

But here's what makes her story truly magical: It's not about the billions she earned or the records she broke. It's about the extraordinary power of not giving up when everything seems hopeless. It's about turning your deepest pain into your greatest strength. It's about believing in your dreams even when no one else does—including yourself.

Are you ready to learn how one ordinary woman created extraordinary magic? Let's dive into this inspiring journey that proves that failure isn't the opposite of success—it is its stepping stone.

The Girl Who Dared to Dream

Born on July 31, 1965, in Yate, England (the same birthday she later shared with Harry Potter—coincidence? I think not!), Joan was the daughter of ordinary, hardworking parents. Her father, Peter, worked as an aircraft engineer, and her mother, Ann, was a science technician. They weren't wealthy, but they were full of love and imagination.

As soon as Joan could hold a pencil, she started making up stories. At six years old, she wrote her first one about a rabbit named "Rabbit" (yes, she admits the title wasn't very creative!). But what mattered wasn't the title—it was her growing passion for storytelling and her desire to create worlds that existed only in her imagination.

Here What I love about this: From childhood, Joan understood a profound thing that many adults forget—that imagination isn't just child's play. It's the birthplace of every great achievement, every breakthrough, every moment when someone changes the world.

Her teachers soon noticed her talent. She read books like she needed them to breathe, losing herself in stories for hours. Most importantly, she was already learning the discipline of writing—something that would later help her when everything else in her life fell apart.

Think about your childhood dreams for a moment. What did you love doing when no one was watching? What made you lose track of time? Joan's story reminds us that those early interests aren't just phases—they often guide us toward who we're meant to become.

The Education of a Future Global Achiever

At Exeter University, Joan studied French and Classics. These subjects might seem unrelated to fantasy writing, but they actually helped her build her magical world. The myths, languages, and cultural stories she learned became part of the rich background of the wizarding world.

But this was where life gave her the first big disappointment: she didn't get admission into Oxford. The rejection hurt. She had imagined walking the same halls as famous writers, studying in a place she had dreamed about for years. Instead, found herself at Exeter—which felt like a second choice to her.

This is your first life lesson from Joan's journey: sometimes what seems like rejection is actually redirection. Oxford may have been prestigious, but Exeter gave her something more valuable—a hunger to prove herself, a determination to create something extraordinary despite not having the "perfect" credentials.

After university, she worked different jobs—first as a researcher at Amnesty International (where she witnessed stories of human courage that would later influence her writing), and later as a secretary in Manchester. But in quiet moments, during lunch breaks or weekend mornings, she was always writing. Always creating. Always believing that someday, somehow, those stories would matter.

The pattern of a success story was already emerging: talent + persistence + unwavering belief in one's vision, even when the world didn't recognize it.

When Life Breaks You

Then came 1990—the year that nearly destroyed Joan, but also gave birth to Harry Potter.

Her mother, Ann her anchor and greatest supporter, was dying of multiple sclerosis. Joan watched helplessly as this vibrant, intelligent woman slowly faded. The grief was overwhelming. The helplessness was crushing. She was only 25 and losing the one person who had always believed in her dreams.

It happened during a delayed train journey from Manchester to London. As she sat there, emotionally drained and exhausted, a story began to unfold in her mind. A boy with messy black hair and green eyes. A boy who didn't know he was special. A boy living with relatives who didn't want him—much like she herself had recently felt unwanted by life.

Here's the real magic: Harry Potter was born not from joy, but from pain. The story that would ultimately bring joy to millions emerged from Joan's darkest moment. This teaches us something profound about the creative process and human resilience – our greatest work often comes not in spite of our suffering, but from how we rise above it.

But life hadn't stopped testing her.

Descent into Darkness

In 1992, seeking a fresh start, Joan moved to Portugal to teach English. There, she met Jorge Arantes, a journalist. They fell in love, married, and had a daughter, Jessica. For a brief moment, it seemed as if life was offering her a happy ending.

But the fairy tale quickly crumbled. The marriage was troubled from the start. Jorge was abusive. Fights were terrible. The atmosphere was toxic. In 1993, when baby Jessica was barely one year old, Joan made the bold decision to leave. She packed up her daughter and her few belongings and returned to Britain.

What awaited her there was poverty she had never imagined.

She moved to Edinburgh to live with her sister, but found herself in a one-bedroom flat with no job, no money, and no hope. She was living on welfare benefits of just £70 a week. She couldn't afford heating. She couldn't afford new clothes. Some days, she couldn't afford food.

Listen to her own words: "I was as poor as you can be in modern Britain without being homeless." Can you imagine? This future billionaire was counting pennies to buy milk for her daughter.

> *"I was as poor as you can be in modern Britain without being homeless."*

Life lessons were harsh but necessary. She learned that rock bottom isn't the end of the story—it's the foundation on which you build your comeback. She discovered that when you have nothing left to lose, you're finally free to risk everything for your dreams.

Cafe Chronicles: Where Magic Was Born

With no money for heating, Joan would wrap baby Jessica in a stroller and walk to cafés in Edinburgh. She would order a cup of coffee and sit there writing for hours. The Elephant House, Nicolson's Café, Deacon's House—these became her offices, her sanctuaries, her writing workshops.

Imagine this scene: a young mother, tired, perhaps wearing the same clothes for the third day, bent over a notebook, completely absorbed in creating a world where an orphan boy discovers he is extraordinary. While other customers chatted about their day jobs and weekend plans, Joan was building Hogwarts, imaginary brick by brick.

The beautiful irony was this: even though she felt like the least magical person in the world, she was creating one of the most magical stories of our time.

She wrote everything by hand because she couldn't afford a typewriter. She plotted the entire seven-book series on scraps of paper. She created character backgrounds, drew maps, invented spells—all while worrying about how she would pay next month's rent.

This phase of her inspiring journey teaches us something important: great work doesn't require perfect conditions. It requires commitment, consistency, and the courage to continue even when every logical voice in your head is screaming "quit."

The Rejection Collection

By 1995, Joan had completed "Harry Potter and the Philosopher's Stone." She typed the manuscript on an old typewriter (yes, she finally managed one), made photocopies, and began sending it to publishers.

Then the rejections started coming. One after another.

Twelve publishers rejected Harry Potter. Twelve! These weren't even form letters—they were specific rejections telling her that the story was too long, too complex, that children wouldn't be interested in such a detailed fantasy world.

One publisher told her she should find a day job because she would never make money from children's books.

Another said the story was "too British" and wouldn't work internationally.

Imagine how she must have felt. Here she was, a single mother living in poverty, pouring her heart and soul into this story, and the publishing world was essentially telling her it was worthless.

But this is where J.K. Rowling's character truly shines: she didn't just collect rejections—she learned from them. She revised, improved, and kept believing. In her own words: *"I never gave up because I knew I had something special, even when no one else could see it."*

> *"I never gave up because I knew I had something special, even when no one else could see it."*

This is the defining moment of any failure-to-success story. It's not about avoiding rejection—it's about how you respond to it. Do you let it crush your dreams, or do you let it fuel your determination?

The Breakthrough That Changed Everything

In 1996, a small London publisher named Bloomsbury finally said yes. But even then, success wasn't guaranteed. Editor Barry Cunningham gave Joan some advice that was both encouraging and sobering: *"You'll never make money from children's books."* He offered her a tiny advance of £1,500 (about $2,500) and suggested she find a day job.

"You'll never make money from children's books."

Joanne's response? She took the money and continued writing.

When "Harry Potter and the Philosopher's Stone" was published in June 1997, the first print run was just 1,000 copies. It went to 500 libraries. It was so small-scale that Joan's name was printed as "J.K. Rowling" instead of "Joanne" because the publisher thought boys wouldn't read a book by a female author.

But then something magical happened.

Children started reading it. Then they started talking about it. Then they started demanding the next book. Word spread from child to child, parent to parent, teacher to teacher. The book that had been rejected by twelve publishers was becoming a phenomenon.

The life lessons here are priceless: Sometimes the biggest breakthroughs come from the smallest beginnings. Sometimes the very thing that makes your work "different"—the very thing that once got you rejected—is exactly what makes it special.

The Meteoric Rise of a Global Phenomenon

What followed was unprecedented in publishing history. The second book, "The Chamber of Secrets," became the fastest-selling novel in UK history at the time. The third book broke that record. By the fourth book, bookstores were holding midnight release parties. Kids were camping out to get copies.

Hollywood soon came calling. Warner Bros. bought the film rights, and suddenly Joan's imaginary world was transforming into a multi-billion-dollar franchise. The first movie, released in 2001, earned $93.5 million in its opening weekend alone.

But what I find most inspiring about this phase of her success story is this: Joan never forgot where she came from. She insisted that movies be filmed in Britain with British actors. She demanded creative control over her characters. She ensured that the stories stayed true to her vision.

When Forbes declared her the world's first billionaire author in 2004, she was simultaneously writing checks to charity. She donated so much money—over £160 million—that Forbes actually removed her from its billionaire list in 2012. She literally gave away her billionaire status.

Think about that for a moment. Most people struggle their entire lives to accumulate wealth. Joan accumulated it so she could give it away.

Numbers That Tell an Extraordinary Story

Now let's take a look at the scale of J.K. Rowling's achievements.

- 500+ million books sold worldwide (by 2023)
- Translated into 80+ languages - more than almost any other author in history
- $7.7+ billion earned from the Harry Potter film franchise
- First author to become a billionaire solely from book sales
- £820 million current net worth despite giving away hundreds of millions

But more than numbers, consider the cultural impact:

- Entire generations of children who learned to love reading because of Harry Potter
- A theme park in Orlando that brings magic to life
- A Broadway play that won 9 Olivier Awards
- Countless young writers who were inspired to create their own stories
- A global community united by a shared love for these characters

This is what true success looks like - when your work doesn't just make you wealthy, but also makes the world a little more magical.

The Leadership Philosophy That Built an Empire

What made J.K. Rowling not just a successful author but a global achiever and cultural leader? Her approach to success reveals some profound principles:

1. Creativity paired with discipline: She didn't just have good ideas—she had the discipline to fully develop them. She plotted seven books in advance, created detailed backstories for minor characters, and built an entire magical universe with consistent rules.

2. Authenticity over marketability: When publishers wanted to change her vision, she fought back. She insisted on British terminology in her books. She refused to dumb down complex themes. Her authenticity is why her stories resonate across cultures.

3. Courage in the Face of Criticism: Religious groups attacked the books for promoting witchcraft. Literary critics dismissed them as "not real literature." Joan continued to write what she believed in.

4. Social Responsibility: As her wealth increased, so did her generosity. She founded *Lumos*, an organization dedicated to ending the institutionalization of children around the world. As she often says, "When we have more than we need, it becomes our moral duty to use that surplus wisely and with compassion."

> *"When we have more than we need, it becomes our moral duty to use that surplus wisely and compassionately."*

This combination—creative vision, unwavering authenticity, moral courage, and social responsibility—is what transforms individual success into a lasting legacy.

Controversies and How She Dealt with Them

No inspirational journey is without its challenges, and Joan has faced her share of controversies in recent years, particularly around social issues. Instead of avoiding difficult topics or simply agreeing with popular opinion, she has consistently spoken her mind, even when it costs her fans and friendships.

What can we learn from this? True leadership sometimes means standing alone. It means having the courage to express your beliefs even when they are unpopular. Whether you agree with her specific positions or not, you must respect her willingness to risk her reputation for her principles.

This teaches us something crucial about authentic success: it's not about being loved by everyone—it's about staying true to yourself and your values, even when it's difficult.

The Writing Process That Created Magic

How did Joan actually create these beloved stories? Her creative process offers insights for anyone trying to build something meaningful:

She started with character, not plot: Harry came to her first—a lonely boy who didn't know he was special. The magical world grew around her, not the other way around.

She planned obsessively: those napkins and scraps of paper from her café days? They contained detailed plots for all seven books, character genealogies, Quidditch statistics, magical creature classifications. She had built entire worlds before writing the first sentence.

She wrote about what she knew: themes of loss, abandonment, the search for belonging, the battle between good and evil—these came from her own experiences with grief, poverty, and moral choices.

She never compromised on quality: even after becoming successful, she continued to revise and perfect her work. Later books are longer and more complex because she refused to dumb them down for commercial success.

Lesson? Great work comes from the intersection of imagination and preparation, creativity and craftsmanship, personal truth and universal themes.

Life Lessons from the Boy Who Lived (and the Woman Who Created Him)

J.K. Rowling's success story offers profound life lessons that extend far beyond writing:

Lesson 1: Your Lowest Point Can Be Your Starting Point

Harry Potter was born from Joan's darkest period—unemployment, divorce, single motherhood, poverty, depression. What seemed like the end of her story was actually the beginning of her greatest chapter.

Application: When you're facing your own dark night of the soul, ask yourself: "What is this experience teaching me? How can this pain become my purpose?"

> *"What is this experience teaching me? How can this pain become my purpose?"*

Lesson 2: Rejection is Redirection, Not Reflection

Twelve publishers said no to Harry Potter. If Joan had believed them, the world would never have known the magic of Hogwarts.

Application: Every "no" is one step closer to your "yes." Keep track of your rejections—they're proof that you're trying, not proof that you're failing.

Lesson 3: Excellence Requires Preparation

Joan didn't just have one good idea—she had seven books' worth of good ideas, all planned out, all interconnected, all consistent with her created world.

Application: Whatever you're building, invest in preparation. Success isn't just about the final product—it's about the foundation on which you build it.

Lesson 4: Success is what you give, not what you get.

Joan gave away her billionaire status through charitable donations. Her legacy isn't her wealth—it's the millions of children who learned to love reading because of her stories.

Application: True fulfillment comes from contribution. How can you use your success to help others succeed?

Lesson 5: Authenticity is more important than perfection.

Joan's stories work because they're honest about difficult topics—death, prejudice, corruption, the complexity of human nature. She didn't sanitize her vision for mass appeal.

Application: Don't try to be what you think others want you to be. Be authentically, courageously yourself.

Ripple Effect: How One Woman's Dream Changed the World

Consider the global impact of J.K. Rowling's unwavering dedication:

- Teachers around the world report that the Harry Potter books helped reluctant readers discover a love of literature.

- Libraries saw a massive increase in children's book borrowing after the Harry Potter series became popular.
- Independent bookstores experienced a renaissance as families found a place to discuss and buy books.
- Young writers found inspiration to create their own fantasy worlds.
- Parents and children found shared stories that brought families together.

This is the power of one person's commitment to their vision. Joan didn't just create entertainment—she created a cultural phenomenon that made reading cool again, brought families together, and inspired countless other creators.

Current Chapter: Still Writing, Still Inspiring

Even today, J.K. Rowling continues to write, both under her own name and under the pseudonym Robert Galbraith (yes, she still faces the challenge of gender bias in publishing). She has expanded the wizarding world with new stories, runs a successful charitable foundation, and continues to speak out on important issues.

But perhaps most importantly, she continues to prove that success isn't a destination—it's a continuous journey of growth, contribution, and authenticity.

Her current net worth of £820 million could be much higher if she hadn't given so much away. But that's the point. She has redefined what it means to be successful. It's not about accumulating wealth—it's about using your gifts to make a positive difference.

Your Magical Journey Begins Now

So, what does J.K. Rowling's inspiring journey mean to you?

Perhaps you're sitting in your own metaphorical café, working on a dream that others don't understand. Perhaps you're collecting your own rejection letters, wondering if you're deluding yourself. Perhaps you're at your own rock bottom, wondering if you'll ever be able to climb back up.

Here's what Joan's story teaches us: Your current circumstances are not your final destination. Your rejections are not your reality. Your failures are not your future.

The magic isn't in having perfect conditions—it's in working with whatever conditions you have. The magic isn't in avoiding rejection—it's in persisting despite rejection. The magic isn't in becoming wealthy—it's in becoming someone who can create value for others.

Failure to success isn't just a phrase—it's a process. And that process starts with a simple decision: the decision to keep going even when quitting seems logical, to keep believing even when doubt seems reasonable, to keep creating even when giving up seems sensible.

Joan Rowling made that decision in a cold Edinburgh apartment, with a crying baby and a pile of rejection letters. She did it in café after café, page after page, day after day. She did it 12 times when publishers said no. She did it when critics attacked her work. She does it every time she sits down to write something new.

Now it's your turn to make that decision.

Interactive Challenge: Cast Your Own Magic Spell

Ready to apply J.K. Rowling's life lessons to your inspirational journey? Here are some practical challenges that will help you channel your inner wizard:

Imagination Exercise (Week 1)
Just like young Joan who wrote stories about rabbits, reconnect with your creative spirit:

- **Daily Practice:** Write for 15 minutes every day, even when it's terrible.
- **Dream Big**: What would you create if you knew you couldn't fail?
- **Document Everything:** Carry a notebook like Joan into those cafes.

Persistence Challenge (Week 2)
Time to build your rejection resilience:

- **Count your NOs:** Start a "rejection collection" - apply somewhere, submit your work somewhere, ask for something you want.
- **Reframe failure:** Write about your past "failure" and identify what it taught you.
- **Keep going:** When you feel like quitting on something important, just do it another day.

Preparation Project (Week 3)
Channel Joan's obsessive planning:

- **Map your world:** Whether it's a business plan, a creative project, or a life goal, create a detailed roadmap.

- **Study your heroes:** Research a successful person in your field - what preparation did they do?
- **Build Your Foundation:** What skills, knowledge, or resources do you need to develop?

Contribution Challenge (Week 4)
Remember, true magic is what you give to others:

- **Teach someone:** Share one of your skills with someone who needs it.
- **Support a cause:** Even if you're not wealthy, how can you contribute to something you care about?
- **Inspire others:** Tell someone about their potential, talent, or worth.

Reflection Questions for Your Journey:

- What "rejection" in your life could actually be redirected toward something better?
- If you were living in poverty like Joan, but could still pursue your dream, what would that dream be?
- What would you create if you knew it would help millions of people, even if you never got the credit?
- How can you use your current struggles as material for your future success?
- What one small step can you take today toward your "impossible" dream?

The magic word is "start."

J.K. Rowling's story isn't just about writing books or making money. It's about the extraordinary power of ordinary people who refuse to accept "impossible" as an answer.

She teaches us that magic isn't about possessing special powers—it's about the special courage that allows you to continue even when everything seems hopeless.

Your story is still being written. Your magic is still waiting to be discovered. Your Harry Potter could be your business idea, your artistic vision, your social cause, your invention, your family legacy, or your contribution to your community.

But there's one thing about magic—it only works if you believe in it enough to act on it.

So, grab your metaphorical wand (or pen, or keyboard, or paintbrush, or business plan), find your café (or garage, or spare bedroom, or corner of the kitchen table), and start creating the magic the world is waiting for.

Because somewhere out there, someone is waiting for exactly what you have to offer. Someone needs the story only you can tell, the solution only you can provide, the inspiration only you can give.

Magic begins the moment you begin.

Your Hogwarts letter has arrived. It's not coming by owl—it's coming from that voice inside you that whispers, "What if?" and "Maybe I could..." and "I have this idea..."

That voice? It's an invitation to your own magical journey.

Will you accept it?

The adventure of your lifetime awaits. Just as Joanne Rowling discovered in that cold Edinburgh café, sometimes the most magical thing you can do is simply not give up on yourself.

Your story is just beginning. Make it magical.

"It's our choices, Harry, that show who we truly are, far more than our abilities." - Albus Dumbledore (and J.K. Rowling)

The choice is yours. Choose Magic. Choose Courage. Choose to begin.

Chapter 6

Daaji (India) Heart to Heart: From a Village to a Global Revolution

Photo: Heartfulness Photos/CC BY-SA 2.0/Wikimedia Commons–https://commons.wikimedia.org/wiki/File:Kamlesh_D_Patel_(Daaji).jpg, retrieved on 12-11-2025

From Pharmacist and Entrepreneur to Global Spiritual Guide – A Journey that will Change Your Life

Do you also have extraordinary potential hidden within you?

Today we take you on a journey that is not just one person's story, but a roadmap for awakening your hidden extraordinary potential. A ray of hope for every person who is in search of true peace, success, and contentment.

"Whatever you do, make it spiritual. Your heart will guide you."— Kamlesh D. Patel (Daaji)

"Whatever you do, make it spiritual. Your heart will guide you."

"What is needed to touch 4 million hearts in 160 countries? How does a person look like, who gains huge success and still chooses to serve humanity?"

Close your eyes and imagine this for a moment: a 19-year-old boy from a small village in Gujarat sits in quiet meditation, completely unaware that he is taking the first step on a journey that will transform millions of lives worldwide. That boy was Kamlesh D. Patel – fondly known as Daaji across the world today.

This isn't just another success story. It's a saga of grit, wisdom, and an unwavering faith in the transformative power of the human soul. It's the inspiring journey of a man who gained material prosperity in America, built a successful career in pharmacy, and then chose the most precious thing of all—service for the spiritual evolution of humanity.

Today, as you read these words, his legacy continues to spread across continents, touching lives in ways that statistics can never fully capture.

A Rooted Story – When the Ordinary Revealed the Extraordinary

The Seeds of Greatness: A Village Boy's Beginning

September 28, 1956 – In the quiet village of Kalla, Gujarat, a child was born who would one day become a spiritual guide to millions. But there was nothing extraordinary that day – no shooting stars, no divine signs. Just a child born into an ordinary family, with seeds of compassion in his heart that would later blossom into a global movement.

Growing up in Kalla, little Kamlesh was like any other village child, yet there was something different – something only time future would reveal. While other children played, he found himself lost in moments of quiet contemplation. While others pursued material dreams, he was drawn to something deeper, something that whispered of meaning beyond the visible world.

"I was always curious," said Daaji, not just about how things work, but about why we exist, what our purpose is.It wasn't the curiosity of someone who doubted everything, but the deep quest of a soul that felt there were more mysteries in life.

> *"I was always curious, not just about how things work, but about why we exist, what our purpose is."*

His family, though modest in means, was rich in values. They taught him the importance of education, hard work, and service to others. These weren't just spoken lessons—they were principles lived daily. In this nurturing environment, young Kamlesh discovered first lesson of life: true wealth isn't measured in rupees or dollars, but in the love, we share and the lives we impact.

The Incident that Changed his Life

Young Kamlesh's spiritual curiosity was so strong that he once set out in search of God. He thought, "If I want to know the truth, I must meet someone who knows it."

> *"If I want to know the truth, I must meet someone who knows it."*

In his search, he met a monk. Young Kamlesh expressed his desire: "I too want to become a monk. I will come with you."

The monk looked at him deeply and gave a simple but profound answer: "I have not yet seen God, and now it is so late that I cannot return home even if I wanted to. Son, return home. Find a suitable path. True spirituality is not found in the forest, but in the midst of life."

> *"True spirituality is not found in the forest, but in the midst of life."*

This sentence became a turning point in life of Kamlesh. He realized that the real challenge was not to take renunciation, but to live a spiritual life while living in the world.

At 19: When He Found his Path

At the age of 19, while studying pharmacy at the L.M. College of Pharmacy in Ahmedabad, something remarkable happened. At the urging of a friend, Kamlesh met a meditation trainer and experienced Sahaj Marg meditation (Presently known as Heartfulness), which was transmission-based. This was the moment when his life found direction.

Combining the scientific study of pharmacy and the ancient science of meditation was no easy task. But Kamlesh understood that true healing lays not in mere physical medicine, but in peace of mind—in touching the essence of human existence.

He saw no contradiction between scientific inquiry and spiritual exploration. In fact, he believed they were complementary paths to understanding the mysteries of life.

"You are the experiment, you are the experimenter, and you are the result" Daaji says, adopting this philosophy even as a young student. This wasn't just a saying—it was the foundation of an approach to spirituality that would revolutionize the way millions connect with their inner selves.

"You are the experiment, you are the experimenter, and you are the result"

Realization of the American Dream:

Material Success with a Spiritual Foundation

With a pharmacy degree, Kamlesh moved to the United States in 1980. The decision wasn't easy. An unknown country, a different culture, a new language—everything was challenging.

Like other countless immigrants, he came with dreams of success, but unlike many others, he also brought an unwavering commitment to his spiritual practice—a combination that would prove to be his greatest strength.

The America of the 1980s was a land of opportunities. But it was also a place where dreams could be crushed as easily as they were born. For a young man from a village in Gujarat, the culture shock was immense. Everything was different—the pace of life, the values, the way people connected with each other. Yet, Kamlesh possessed something that set him apart: the inner stability that came from a regular meditation practice.

Visualize Kamlesh in those early days, working long hours in American pharmacies, his Indian accent is attracting curious glances, his traditional values seemingly out of place in a materialistic society. But what makes his story extraordinary is this: instead of abandoning his spiritual roots to fit in, he used them as the foundation to build remarkable material success.

The struggles were deep. First came professional challenges—proving himself in a competitive environment, overcoming language barriers, adapting to different work cultures. But Kamlesh had discovered something powerful: when you approach material challenges with spiritual intelligence, solutions emerge that benefit everyone.

His colleagues began to see something different in him. Here was someone who worked with complete dedication yet remained detached from results. Someone who pursued excellence without being driven by ego. Someone who could handle pressure with remarkable calm and find creative solutions that others missed.

"I was caught," Daaji later shared, "between the pursuit of material success and my deep spiritual quest." But what he discovered was revolutionary: there was no real conflict between the two when approached from the heart. His meditation practice didn't hinder his professional growth—it accelerated it, giving him clarity, creativity, and the ability to build genuine relationships with colleagues and customers.

"I was caught between the pursuit of material success and my deep spiritual quest."

Within a few years, Kamlesh had established himself as a highly successful pharmacist. His expertise was in demand, his advice valued, his leadership recognized. He had achieved what many only dare to dream of—financial security, professional respect, and the realization of the American dream. But unlike many who find material success empty, Kamlesh's achievement was deeply satisfying because it was built on a foundation of inner peace and service to others.

Night after night, in his comfortable American home—a world away from his modest village beginnings, Kamlesh sat in meditation, not as an escape from material success, but as the practice that truly made that success meaningful. These weren't just meditation sessions—they were a daily renewal of his connection with purpose, the source of the wisdom that guided his business decisions, and the foundation of the peace he radiated wherever he went.

What sustained him during these successful years was a growing awareness, his material achievements were preparing him for something greater. Every challenge he overcame in the business world was developing the abilities he would later need as a global spiritual leader.

Guiding Light: The Guidance that Changed Everything

Babuji and Chariji: Life-Changing Meetings

Behind every great man are great guides, and Kamlesh's journey was blessed by two extraordinary guides. The first was Shri Ram Chandra, fondly called Babuji, founder of the Shri Ram Chandra Mission (now popularly known as Heartfulness Institute). The second was P. Rajgopalachari, fondly called Chariji, Babuji's successor and the Mission's second president.

Meeting Babuji was not just a meeting—it was a soul-searching. Babuji's philosophy was revolutionary: "Spirituality is not for those who live in caves, but for ordinary people living ordinary lives."

> *"Spirituality is not for those who live in caves, but for ordinary people living ordinary lives."*

"The relationship between a spiritual guide and a seeker," Daaji explained, "is not about dependency, but about awakening the guide within."

After Babuji's passing, Chariji became Kamlesh's mentor, continuing the work of nurturing this young seeker destined for great things. Chariji saw in Kamlesh a rare combination of intellectual precision and heart-centered wisdom. Here was someone who could build bridges between ancient and modern, Eastern and Western, science and spirituality.

Under Chariji's guidance, Kamlesh learned the most important lesson of his life: leadership in the spiritual realm is not about commanding from above, but about serving from within. A true leader does not create followers, but awakens other leaders. This lesson would later become the foundation of his approach to leading the Heartfulness movement.

"Whatever you do, make it spiritual. Your heart will guide you," this quote became more than just a teaching—it became a way of life. Whether working in a pharmacy in America or meditating in India, Kamlesh learned to infuse every task with spiritual awareness.

2011 – When Life Took a New Turn

From Successor to Leader

2011 was a turning point that would change everything. Chariji, recognizing the divine qualities that had been nurtured in Kamlesh over decades, named him his successor. But this wasn't just a transfer of power—it was a call to responsibility, the recognition of a soul ready to serve humanity at the highest level.

Imagine that moment. Kamlesh, at 55, was told he was now to lead a global spiritual movement. Leaving behind the comfortable life he had built in America and returning to India to lead a global spiritual movement that was already touching millions of lives was a daunting task. It wasn't just a career change—it was a complete transformation of identity and purpose.

This decision must not have been easy. He had established himself professionally in America, built a comfortable life there, and cultivated a sense of security. But the call to service was stronger than the allure of comfort. In 2014, after handing over his business to his children, Kamlesh officially became the Global Guide of the Heartfulness movement. The world came to know him as "Daaji."

Daaji didn't approach his new role with the arrogance of someone who had "made it" or the fear of someone who felt unprepared. Instead, he brought the humility of a lifelong seeker and the wisdom of someone who understood that true leadership was about empowering others to find their own greatness.

“Without peace, we cannot be creative,” he often said, and this became the guiding principle of his leadership. Under his guidance, the Heartfulness movement began to evolve in ways that surprised even long-time practitioners.

“Without peace, we cannot be creative,”

Kamlesh's transformation from pharmacist to Global Guide did not happen overnight. It was the natural blossoming of decades of inner work, years of service, and a lifetime of preparation. But when the moment came, he stepped into his role not with ambition, but with love—love for the practices that had transformed his own life and love for the millions of others seeking the same transformation.

Building Dreams: The Vision of Kanha Shanti Vanam

"Dreams" are the blueprints for reality and Daaji's dream was as ambitious as it was beautiful: to create a place where people from all walks of life could come together to experience peace, inner joy, transformation, and spiritual awakening. This dream took the form of Kanha Shanti Vanam, which became the world's largest meditation center.

Imagine: 1,200 acres of pristine barren land near Hyderabad, transformed into a green heaven planted with one million trees that could accommodate 100,000 meditators simultaneously. But it wasn't just about size—it was about creating an environment where the very atmosphere supported inner transformation. Every tree planted, every building constructed, every path designed was imbued with the intention of facilitating spiritual growth.

The construction of Kanha Shanti Vanam faced many challenges. There were practical hurdles—obtaining permits, managing construction, coordinating with local authorities. There were financial challenges—funding such a massive project without compromising the fact that meditation should always be offered free of charge. Creating infrastructure that could handle large gatherings while maintaining the sanctity of the place.

But Daaji took every challenge not as a problem to be solved, but as an opportunity to demonstrate the power of collective intention. Thousands of volunteers from around the world contributed their time, skills, and resources. What emerged was not just a meditation center, but a testament to what is impossible when people unite around a shared vision of human transformation.

From Barren Land to Green Paradise: A Miracle of Nature

When Daaji first saw this land, it was completely barren and dry. There was a lack of water, rocky soil, and not a single green tree in sight. The locals said, "Nothing can grow on this land."

But Daaji had a different perspective. He said: "The soil that can blossom the flower of peace in millions of hearts can also grow green trees and plants."

> *"The soil that can blossom the flower of peace in millions of hearts can also grow green trees and plants."*

Today, that same land has become a green paradise. Rainwater was harvested using unique water conservation techniques. Organic farming methods made the soil fertile. And most importantly, each tree was planted with the love of one's own child.

Recognition of National Leaders: When Even the Highest Positions Bowed

President Ram Nath Kovind's Historic Visit (2020)

In February 2020, the President of India, Ram Nath Kovind, visited Kanha Shanti Vanam. This was the first official visit by an Indian President to a meditation center. His words were deeply moving:

"This complex presents a model of holistic living. It is a great place for spiritual renewal. The activities carried out here for the benefit of women, farmers, and small entrepreneurs are commendable."

President Kovind further said: "The peace and positive energy here are amazing. This place is not only for personal transformation, but also a hub for social change."

President Draupadi Murmu's Blessings (2024)
President Draupadi Murmu's presence at the Global Spirituality Festival in 2024 will elevate the movement to new heights. She said, "The work of Heartfulness is an important step towards global peace and human unity. This movement, led by Daaji, is an inspiration not only for India but for the entire world."

Vice President Jagdeep Dhankhar's support (2024)
Vice President Jagdeep Dhankhar also participated in the same event and said:

"Kanha Shanti Vanam symbolizes the beautiful synthesis of spirituality and science in the modern age. This place is playing an important role in guiding the youth in the right direction."

Prime Minister Narendra Modi's inspiring message
Prime Minister Narendra Modi praised Daaji's work, saying:

"Under Daaji's spiritual leadership, the Shri Ram Chandra Mission is inspiring the entire world. The Heartfulness program is like a ray of hope for the world. It presents India's spiritual heritage in a modern context."

The Prime Minister further said: "Heartfulness's contribution in bringing ancient Indian traditions like yoga and meditation to the global stage is incomparable."

Union Environment Minister Special Mention by Bhupendra Yadav

At Daaji's 70th birthday celebrations, Union Minister for Environment, Forest and Climate Change Bhupendra Yadav said: *"Work of Daaji and Heartfulness is amazing. They are working on both peace of mind and environmental conservation. By planting the millionth tree, he proved that spiritual development and environmental conservation are complementary to each other."*

The Minister further said: "The 'Forest by Heartfulness' initiative has set a new standard in environmental conservation. It shows that spiritual awareness naturally leads to environmental responsibility."

View of Yoga Guru Baba Ramdev

Yoga Guru Baba Ramdev praised Daaji's work, saying:

"Daaji has taken yoga and meditation to new heights. The Heartfulness method is simple, scientific, and effective. It is an ideal model of spirituality for the modern age."

Baba Ramdev further said: "Kanha Shanti Vanam is a symbol of India's spiritual strength. The peace experienced here is unparalleled."

International Recognition and Views from Global Leaders

United Nations Honors

The United Nations Department of Public Information recognized Heartfulness as a partner organization. UN officials said:

"Heartfulness is making a significant contribution to global peace and the achievement of the Sustainable Development Goals. Daaji's approach is inclusive and transformative."

Commonwealth Global Ambassador (2024)
In 2024, Daaji was appointed the Commonwealth's Global Ambassador for Peacebuilding and Faith. The Commonwealth Secretary-General said:

"Under Daaji's leadership, Heartfulness has demonstrated how spirituality can become a vehicle for social harmony and peace. His work is inspiring to the Commonwealth family of 56 countries."

Padma Bhushan Award (2023)
In 2023, the Government of India honored Daaji with the Padma Bhushan – one of India's highest civilian honors. The award ceremony stated:

"Kamlesh D. Patel (Daaji) has made incomparable contributions to spirituality and social work. His life is a living example of service and dedication."

Unity in Diversity: The Magic of Kanha Shanti Vanam

If you want to witness a miracle, visit Kanha Shanti Vanam during any major spiritual gathering. Here, something extraordinary happens that challenges our thinking about human differences and divisions.

Imagine it: millions of people from every corner of the world—of different nations, castes, religions, economic backgrounds, ages, and professions—sitting together in perfect harmony, united in silence, connected by the invisible threads of the heart.

This isn't just a beautiful ideal—it's a living reality that Daaji has made possible through the power of heart-centered unity. At these gatherings, you'll see a CEO from New York sitting next to a farmer from rural India, a professor from Germany meditating with a student from Africa, elderly practitioners sharing space and thoughts with children—all proof that all boundaries dissolve in the shared experience of inner peace.

Global Media Reaction
The BBC wrote in a special report on Kanha Shanti Vanam:

"This place is a unique experiment in the modern world, where people from different cultures come together without any discrimination. What Daaji has created is a living model of global unity."

The New York Times wrote:
"Kanha Shanti Vanam is not just a meditation center—it is a social movement that proves that spirituality transcends boundaries."

"In the silence of the heart," Daaji explains, "all differences fade away. What remains is the recognition that we are all part of the same human family, all seeking the same fundamental things—peace, love, and meaning."

Ripple Effect: Global Impact and Transformation

Numbers tell a story, but they cannot capture the full impact of a life dedicated to service. Today, the Heartfulness movement is active in more than 160 countries, with over 4 million practitioners worldwide. These aren't just statistics—these are 4 million stories of personal transformation, 4 million hearts that have found peace through Daaji's teachings.

But how does a movement grow from a village boy's personal practice to a global phenomenon that touches millions of lives? The answer lies in the authenticity of the message and the genuine transformation experienced by practitioners.

Unlike many spiritual movements that rely on charismatic personalities or complex doctrines, Heartfulness spread through the simple power of heart-to-heart transmission. Everyone who experienced transformation naturally wanted to share that experience with others. Every life touched became a beacon for other seekers.

The Impact of the Heartfulness Education Trust

Consider the Heartfulness Education Trust, which has integrated meditation into more than 2,500 schools, universities, and colleges. This isn't about imposing spiritual practices on educational institutions—it's about recognizing that true education involves more than just filling the mind with information, but nurturing the whole human being.

Researchers at Harvard University found in a study:
"Students who practiced Heartfulness meditation had 32% lower stress levels, along with28% improvement in academic performance too."

Environmental Conservation: When Spirituality Became the Green Revolution

"Forest by Heartfulness" Initiative

The "Forest by Heartfulness" initiative, which has planted over 1 million trees with a target of 30 million by 2030, demonstrates how spiritual consciousness naturally leads to environmental consciousness. When you realize that all life is interconnected, caring for the Earth becomes not just a responsibility, but a joy.

The United Nations Environment Programme (UNEP) praised the initiative, saying:

"Heartfulness has shown how spiritual movements can play a vital role in environmental protection. It is an exemplary model."

Global environmentalist Dr. Vandana Shiva said:

"Daaji proved that inner change and outer change are interconnected. When we find peace within ourselves, we naturally want to protect nature."

When Lives Changed - Heartwarming Stories

Daaji's meditation has transformed the lives of people of all ages and backgrounds.

72-year-old Dr. Patricia found renewed energy, Rajesh found relief from corporate stress, Amit found freedom from addiction, and 80-year-old Sumitra Dadi discovered a new meaning in life.

Even world leaders are inspired—Satya Nadella says, "Meditation is part of modern leadership," while Google's Director of Wellbeing believes, "Heartfulness increases both productivity and peace."

Challenges and Wisdom: The Price of Growth

Success, even spiritual success, comes with its own set of challenges. As the Heartfulness movement grew from a small group of practitioners to a global phenomenon, Daaji faced difficulties that took test of his wisdom and resilience.

One of the greatest challenges was maintaining the authenticity and quality of Heartfulness practice as it spread across diverse cultures and communities. How do you ensure that the essence of the teaching remains intact when it is being shared by thousands of trainers in hundreds of countries, each with their own cultural context and understanding?

Daaji's solution was characteristically wise: instead of trying to control from the center, he focused on preparing trainers and empowering trainers to connect with the source within themselves. "A book can give us wisdom, but it cannot make us wise," he taught.True understanding comes not from memorizing instructions, but from experiencing the practice so deeply that you can guide others from authentic experience.

> *"A book can give us wisdom, but it cannot make us wise,"*

Gratitude and Grace: Respect for the Hierarchy of Masters

One of the most beautiful aspects of Daaji's character is his unwavering humility and deep gratitude to his spiritual masters.

Despite achieving global recognition and leading a worldwide movement, he consistently attributes all his success to the guidance and grace of his predecessors—Babuji, Chariji, and the entire Hierarchy of Masters who came before him.

"I am only a medium," he often says with genuine humility. "Whatever transformation occurs through Heartfulness is the result of the wisdom and love passed down by generations of Masters. I am simply grateful to have been chosen as an instrument of their grace."

This attitude is not false humility—it is the authentic identity of someone who understands that personal achievement is always built on the contributions of others.

Qualities of Daaji that make him extraordinary

1. A true medium of inner transformation
Daaji doesn't just talk; he's a living example. His entire life demonstrates how inner transformation can transform the outer world.

2. A ray of hope
Daaji gives hope to those who have despaired, those who have given up. His message is simple: "There's still so much left. It's just a matter of starting."

> *"There's still so much left. It's just a matter of starting."*

3. The ability to evaluate

Daaji always says: "You are the experiment, you are the experimenter, and you are the result." This is the power of self-evaluation that he instills in every practitioner.

4. A living example of humility

Despite all his success, Daaji possesses a humility that wins everyone's heart.

5. A living embodiment of compassion

Remember the story of Amit – when Daaji saw that drunk young man, he didn't preach. Just looked at him with loving eyes. And that one look was enough to change Amit's life. This is the power of compassion.

6. Love that is Unconditional

Daaji's love is unconditional. Whether you are rich or poor, educated or uneducated, young or old—his love is the same for everyone. It is this unconditional love that draws millions to him.

7. Awakening the Inner Guide

Daaji's greatest teaching is that he does not create dependency, but awakens the inner guide in every person. He says: "The answer is not outside, but within you. I am simply showing you the path to meet your inner Master."

> *"The answer is not outside, but within you. I am simply showing you the path to meet your inner Master."*

The Foundation of True Success: Make Meditation Your Pillar

Here comes the most important lesson from Daaji's journey. If you want true success in your material life, make meditation the foundation of your success. Why? Because many people lose their inner peace and inner happiness in pursuit of material success and if you're not peaceful and happy from within, we can't call it true success.

Like Daaji, you too can choose Heartfulness practices that can be easily integrated into your routine life. It's not a complicated process – just 20-30 minutes of simple meditation practice daily can help you unlock your hidden extraordinary potential.

Stanford University research revealed:
"Individuals who regularly practiced Heartfulness meditation experienced a 42% improvement in decision-making, a 38% increase in emotional stability, and a 45% increase in overall life satisfaction."

The Art of Modern Leadership: Where Science Meets Spirituality

What does leadership mean in the 21st century? Daaji's approach offers profound insights that apply far beyond the spiritual realm, demonstrating how ancient wisdom can inform modern challenges.

A Harvard Business School professor said:
"Daaji's leadership model—leadership through service, integrating science and spirituality, and empowering others—is a perfect example of 21st-century leadership."

Your Journey Awaits: A Call to Transformation

As we conclude this inspiring journey of Daaji's life, a question arises: What does his story mean to you? How can the lessons of his path illuminate your own journey toward fulfillment and transformation?

Firstly, remember that every great journey begins with a single step. Daaji's transformation didn't happen overnight—it was the result of decades of consistent practice, continuous learning, and an unwavering commitment to growth.

Secondly, understand that challenges and failures are not obstacles to success—they are the very ingredients from which success is built.

Thirdly, recognize that the true success involves serving something greater than yourself. Daaji's success came not from personal achievement, but from contributing to the transformation of others.

The Heart's Final Word

Daaji's story reminds us that the most profound transformations often begin in those quiet moments when we pause long enough to listen to our hearts. Examples of Einstein and other scientists prove the same fact. In a world that celebrates noise, Daaji chose silence. In a culture that worships material success, he chose service. In an era that promotes individual achievement, he chose collective transformation.

His journey from Kamlesh, a village boy from Gujarat, to Daaji, a global guide to millions, is not just an inspiring success story—it's a roadmap for everyone who wants to live with authenticity, purpose, and impact.

Your journey begins now. Your heart knows the way.

"Whatever you do, make it spiritual. Your heart will guide you."—Daaji

Practical Guidance: How to Begin Your Journey

Seven-Day Heart-Centered Living Challenge:
Day 1 - Practice Presence: Spend 10 minutes in quiet contemplation, focusing on your heart daily and observing your thoughts without judgment.

Day 2 - Serve Others: Perform an act of service without expecting recognition or reward.

Day 3 - Listen Deeply: Have a conversation where you focus on listening to fully understand, not to respond.

Day 4 - Express Gratitude: Write a letter of appreciation to someone who has positively influenced your life.

Day 5 - Face Fear: Take one small step toward something you've been avoiding due to fear or uncertainty.

Day 6 - Connect with Nature: Spend time outdoors, appreciating the natural world and your place in it.

Day 7 - Visualize Your Legacy: Write about the positive impact you want to have on the world and identify one action to move toward that vision.

Reflection Questions for Personal Growth:

1. Village Boy: What childhood dreams did you have that you may have forgotten or put aside? How can reconnecting with that early vision serve your growth today?

2. Crossing the Ocean: What "foreign land" in your life—whether geographical, professional, or personal—has challenged you to discover inner strength you didn't know you possessed?

3. Mentor Question: Who have been the guiding influences in your life? How can you honor their influence while developing your authentic voice and wisdom?

4. Service Challenge: If you knew you couldn't fail, what contribution would you want to make to the world? What is holding you back from taking the first step toward that vision today?

5. Heart vs. Head: In what areas of your life you are making decisions primarily with your head while your heart is trying to guide you in a different direction?

Life Lessons Learned from Daaji

1. Balance the Materiality and the Spirituality: Daaji proved that you don't have to choose between money and peace. Both can coexist.

2. Strength in Humility: The greatest achievements come to those who give rather than take credit.

3. Service is True Success: When you serve others, you find your greatest satisfaction.

4. Inner Work Brings Outer Results: Work within yourself, and the outside world will begin to change.

5. Patience and Perseverance: Great transformations don't happen overnight. They are the result of decades of consistent effort.

Final Message: Your Time is Now

Daaji's story conveys the message that extraordinary talents lie hidden even in ordinary people. You don't need to be born into a privileged family, nor do you need supernatural powers. All you need is:

- A sincere intention – to serve humanity
- Regular practice – daily meditation and self-reflection
- Patience – not rushing for results
- Humility – giving credit for your success to others
- Love – unconditional, for all

The story of a village boy who became a Global guide proves that when there is a true desire in the heart, nothing is impossible.

Start today. Just 20 minutes of meditation. Just one person's sincere help. Just one small step inward.

Daaji showed that the path is possible. Now it's your turn to walk on that path.

Contacts and Resources

Connect with Heartfulness:

- Website: www.heartfulness.org
- Heartfulness App: Free guided meditation
- Find the nearest meditation center/trainer
- Join online sessions
- Visit Kanha Shanti Vanam: Hyderabad, Telangana, India

Remember: This journey is free, open to all, and can be undertaken by people of any religion, caste, or background.

"When you listen to the voice of your heart, the whole universe is ready to help you." — Daaji

"When you listen to the voice of your heart, the whole universe is ready to help you."

Your extraordinary journey begins today. Are you ready?

Ending Note:

This chapter is just a glimpse into Daaji's life. His full story is alive in his life, in his teachings, and in the transformation of millions of people who have practiced Heartfulness.

This isn't just one person's story. It's the story of the potential that lies within every human being. It's the story of the power that comes from love, dedication, and service and most importantly—it could be the beginning of your story.

Daaji has shown the way. Now it's up to you to walk.

Your Complete Transformation Worksheet

Ordinary to Extraordinary

Part 1: Interactive - Your Legend DNA Quiz

Answer honestly (A, B, or C):

1. When you fail at something, you usually:

A) Give up and try something else

B) Feel bad but eventually try again

C) Analyze what went wrong and try differently

2. When people doubt your dreams, you:

A) Start doubting yourself too

B) Feel hurt but keep it to yourself

C) Use it as motivation to prove them wrong

3. Your biggest current challenge is:

A) Fear of failure stopping you from starting

B) Dealing with recent rejection or setback

C) Staying consistent and not giving up

4. If you could ask one legend for advice, you'd ask:

A) "How did you overcome fear?"

B) "How did you handle rejection?"

C) "How did you stay motivated for so long?"

5. Your dream right now feels:

A) Impossible - I'm not sure I can do it

B) Difficult - but maybe possible

C) Challenging - but I'm committed

Your Results:

Mostly A's: You're at the **Starting Line** - You need Edison's mother's belief. Start believing in yourself FIRST.

Mostly B's: You're **Building Momentum** - You need Jobs' comeback spirit. One setback isn't the end of your story.

Mostly C's: You're **On the Path** - You need Ma's persistence. Keep going - your breakthrough is coming.

Part 2: The 6 Legends Challenge

Choose ONE action from each legend to complete this week:

Edison's Challenge: Try something 10 times (not once, not twice - TEN TIMES)

- My 10 attempts will be: ______________________________________
- Start Date: ____________

Jobs' Challenge: Return to something you gave up on

- I will restart: ____
- This week I'll: ____

Ma's Challenge: Hear "NO" without quitting

- I will ask/apply/try for: ______________________________
- Even if rejected, I'll: ______________________________

Rowling's Challenge: Write/create during your struggle

- I will create: ______________________________________
- Time commitment: ____________________________________

Disney's Challenge: Dream bigger than seems realistic

- My "impossible" dream: ______________________________
- First step toward it: ________________________________

Daaji's Challenge: Spend 10 minutes in quiet reflection daily

- Meditation/Reflection time: __________________________
- What I'll reflect on: ________________________________

Part 3: Your Personal Failure-to-Success Map

Document YOUR journey (inspired by all 6 legends):

My Current "Rock Bottom" / Biggest Challenge:

What people are saying I CAN'T do:

My "Impossible" Dream (be bold!):

My First "3,000 Experiments" - What Will I Try Repeatedly?

1. ____________________
2. ____________________
3. ____________________

My Comeback Plan (when I face rejection):

Part 4: The Legend Mindset Shift

Replace these thoughts TODAY:

Old mindset out (Old thinking)	**New mindset in (legend thinking)**
"I'm not smart enough"	" I'm learning."
"I got rejected/fired"	" This is my comeback setup"
"Nobody believes in me"	"I believe in myself"
"I'm too broke to succeed"	" My story is just beginning"
"They said I have no talent"	" They're wrong."
"I don't know my purpose"	" I'm on my purposeful journey

Write your personal mindset shift:

I will stop thinking:

____

I will start believing:

____

Part 5: Your 30-Day Legends Commitment

I commit to embodying these legend traits:

□ **Edison's Persistence** - I will try ______ times before quitting anything

□ **Jobs' Vision** - I will think differently and create

____

□ **Ma's Resilience** - I will handle rejection by

____

□ **Rowling's Faith** - I will keep creating even when

____

□ **Disney's Imagination** - I will dream about

____

□ **Daaji's Purpose** - I will reflect on

____

My 30-Day Focus Goal:

Daily Check-in: Week 1: ○ ○ ○ ○ ○ ○ ○ | Week 2: ○ ○ ○ ○ ○ ○ ○
Week 3: ○ ○ ○ ○ ○ ○ ○ | Week 4: ○ ○ ○ ○ ○ ○ ○

Part 6: Your Legend Letter

Write a letter to yourself from your future successful self (as if you've already made it):

Dear Current Me,

I know right now you're struggling with

____

But I want you to know that

____

Remember when

____

Keep going because

____

The legends proved that

____

You've got this because

____

Signed, Your Future Legendary Self Date: ____________

Part 7: Share Your Legend Journey

The 6 legends changed the world. Now it's YOUR turn.

I will inspire others by: □ Sharing my struggles honestly □ Helping someone who's where I was □ Documenting my journey □ Refusing to give up publicly □ Being proof that comebacks are real

One person I'll share this with:

____

What I'll tell them:

____

Final Commitment Contract

I, _________________________ (your name), have learned from 6 legends that:

- Failure is not final
- Rejection is redirection
- "Impossible" is an opinion
- Persistence beats talent
- My story isn't over
- Success means Peace & happiness also

Therefore, I REFUSE to: □ Give up after one failure □ Let others define my limits □ Believe I'm not enough □ Quit before my breakthrough

And I COMMIT to: □ Trying repeatedly like Edison □ Thinking differently like Jobs □ Persisting endlessly like Ma □ Creating through struggle like Rowling □ Dreaming impossibly like Disney □ Finding purpose like Daaji

Signature: ____________________ **Date:** _________________

Witness (optional): ______________ **Date:** _________________

Remember:

Edison's light bulb moment came after 3,000+ failures. Jobs' iPhone came AFTER being fired. Ma's Alibaba came AFTER 30 rejections. Rowling's Harry Potter came AFTER rock bottom. Disney's empire came AFTER being fired. Daaji's mission came AFTER finding purpose.

Your breakthrough is coming. Don't stop now.

Bonus: Legend Quotes Wall

Pick ONE quote to write somewhere you'll see daily:

"I have not failed. I've found 10,000 ways that won't work." - Edison

"The people who are crazy enough to think they can change the world are the ones who do." - Jobs

"If you don't give up, you still have a chance." - Ma

"Rock bottom became the solid foundation on which I rebuilt my life." - Rowling

"All our dreams can come true if we have the courage to pursue them." - Disney

"Inner transformation leads to outer transformation." - Daaji

My chosen quote:

____

Where I'll place it:

____

Congratulations! You've completed the 6 Legends Journey!

Now go write YOUR legendary story. The world is waiting.

Scan the QR code or tap the link below to join the AspirixWriters community and grow together.

AspirixWriters
WhatsApp channel

https://whatsapp.com/channel/0029VbBngx34CrfexYg7f104

Conclusion

The journey ordinary to extraordinary begins from within

Every great journey begins not from without, but from inner peace. The truth is that extraordinary people are not born—they become extraordinary by discovering themselves.

Every story in this book—whether it's from a dreamer, a successful person, or a seeker—reveals the same truth: when the mind is calm and the heart is open, life itself rises to a higher level. Success, peace, and purpose are not distant things; they are natural consequences of the awakened consciousness that comes from meditation.

Meditation is the bridge that connects you to your true potential. It refines the mind, purifies the heart, and creates an unbreakable balance within. Through Daaji's inspiration, thousands have discovered that true power lies not in control, but in quiet stillness—not in rushing, but in the stillness of within.

Extraordinary lives are not made by luck—they are made with awareness, discipline, compassion, and a purposeful heart. And it all starts with one small step—closing your eyes and going within.

When you close the last page of this book, pause for a moment… breathe… and listen to the silence within you because that's where your extraordinary story begins.

The path to your success begins not outside—but within.

A Small Request

Thank you for reading.

If this book added value to your life, I'd appreciate it if you left an honest review on Amazon. Your feedback helps other readers discover this book and supports independent authors.

About the Authors

Dr. Rekha Khandelwal and CA Ajay Khandelwal

Dr. Rekha and CA Ajay Khandelwal are an inspiring couple who believe in promoting balance, values, and self-development in every aspect of life. Both are certified Heartfulness Meditation trainers and share their life experiences, demonstrating that true success is achieved when external achievements and inner peace go together.

Dr. Rekha Khandelwal is a thoughtful thinker and academician in the field of law. Through her research, she has demonstrated how spirituality and clarity of thought are essential for decision-making and self-development. Her vision inspires young people that success begins with self-awareness.

CA Ajay Khandelwal, a chartered accountant, believes in integrating financial discipline with life's values. He inspires people to understand that when hard work and awareness are combined, every goal is achievable.

Together, they are the founders of AspirixWriters—a platform that helps people pursue self-expression and self-development through writing, education, and inspiration. AspirixWriters aims to empower everyone to discover their inner creativity and transform it into positive influence.

This book, "Pathways to Success," is the result of their shared vision—a journey that demonstrates that success is not just a destination, but a continuous process fueled by self-belief, values, and awareness.

Their aim is to inspire readers to look within, recognize their potential, and move forward in life with a positive attitude.

Connect with the Authors

We'd love to hear your thoughts, experiences, and inspiring stories.

Your feedback encourages us to continue writing and sharing new inspirations.

Our upcoming book,

"[***Pathways to Success - Inspiring Stories of YouTubers and Social Media Icons Who Built Fame from Zero***]"

will be published soon—featuring new inspiring stories of life, creativity, and success. Stay connected and be a part of these inspiring journeys.

If you have an inspiring story of your own and want to share it with others—or want to join us live—please let us know.

Together, we'll spread a new wave of positivity and inspiration.

Connect with us:

- Website: www.aspirixwriters.com
- Instagram: @AspirixWriters
- Facebook: @AspirixWriters
- YouTube: AspirixWriters
- LinkedIn: AspirixWriters
- Medium.com: AspirixWriters
- Pinterest: AspirixWriter

https://aspirixwriters.com/

scan the QR Code or click the link to join AspirixWriters Community

References:

Chapter 1

1. Britannica. (2025, October 13). Thomas Edison | Biography, Early Life, Inventions & Facts. Encyclopedia Britannica. https://www.britannica.com/biography/Thomas-Edison
2. Wikipedia Contributor. (2001, January 22). Thomas Edison. Wikipedia. https://en.wikipedia.org/wiki/Thomas_Edison
3. Library of Congress. (2025, September 30). Life of Thomas Alva Edison | Biography | Articles & Essays. https://www.loc.gov
4. National Park Service. (2015, February 25). Edison Biography - Thomas Edison National Historical Park (U.S. National Park Service). https://www.nps.gov/edis/learn/historyculture/edison-biography.htm
5. Thomas Edison National Historical Park. (2019, December 31). Life of Thomas Edison. ThomasEdison.org. https://thomasedison.org
6. SoftSchools.com. (2004, December 31). Thomas Edison Timeline. https://softschools.com

Chapter 2

1. Editors of Encyclopedia Britannica (2025, October 30). Steve Jobs | Biography, Education, Apple, and Facts. In Encyclopedia Britannica. https://www.britannica.com/biography/Steve-Jobs
2. Editors of Biography.com (2023, May 21). Steve Jobs: Biography, Apple Co-Founder, Entrepreneur. Biography. https://www.biography.com/business-figure/steve-jobs
3. Harvard Business Review (2012, March 31). The Real Leadership Lessons of Steve Jobs. https://hbr.org/2012/04/the-real-leadership-lessons-of-steve-jobs
4. Investopedia (2025, February 2). The Story of Steve Jobs and Apple. https://www.investopedia.com/terms/s/steve-jobs.asp
5. Wikipedia Contributor. (2001, August 15). Steve Jobs. Wikipedia. https://en.wikipedia.org/wiki/Steve_Jobs
6. Steve Jobs Archive. (2010, September 1). Steve Jobs: Build Something Amazing. https://book.stevejobsarchive.com

Chapter 3

1. Business Insider (2025, February 17). Jack Ma's Life: The Billionaire Who Founded Alibaba. https://www.businessinsider.com/jack-ma-alibaba
2. Biography.com Editors (2014, October 1). The Inspiring Life Story of Alibaba Founder Jack Ma. https://www.businessinsider.com/jack-ma-alibaba
3. Britannica (2025, October 11). Jack Ma | Biography, Alibaba, and Facts. Encyclopedia Britannica. https://www.britannica.com/biography/Jack-Ma
4. Wikipedia Contributors (2005, August 10). Jack Ma. Wikipedia. https://en.wikipedia.org/wiki/Jack_Ma
5. Jagran Josh (2020, May 17). Jack Ma's Biography: Birth, Childhood, Education, Philanthropy, Business, and Entertainment Career. https://www.jagranjosh.com/general-knowledge/jack-ma-biography-1589719374-1
6. The University of Hong Kong. (December 31, 2024). Jack Ma Yun - Biography - Honorary Graduate - The University of Hong Kong. https://www4.hku.hk/honorarygraduate/jack-ma-yun-biography
7. World Economic Forum. (2015, January 23). *Jack Ma: I've had lots of failures and rejections | Davos 2015* [Video]. YouTube. https://www.youtube.com/watch?v=1O3ghiyirvU

Chapter 4

1. Britannica Editors. (2025, November 10). J.K. Rowling | Biography, Controversy, Books, Full Name. Encyclopedia Britannica. https://www.britannica.com/biography/J-K-Rowling
2. Wikipedia Contributor. (2001, September 22). J.K. Rowling. Wikipedia. https://en.wikipedia.org/wiki/J._K._Rowling
3. Biography.com Editors. (2021, March 28). J.K. Rowling - Books, Family, and Facts. Biography. https://www.biography.com/writer/jk-rowling
4. Bloomsbury Publishing. (2018, December 31). J.K. Rowling | Author of the Harry Potter Books. Bloomsbury. https://www.bloomsbury.com/author/jk-rowling

5. TEDx Talks. (2011, September 26). *J.K. Rowling: On writing – Part One* [Video]. YouTube. https://www.youtube.com/watch?v=3uLa3WKXwLg

Chapter 5

1. Biography.com Editors (2022, January 6). Walt Disney - Frozen, Quotes & Pictures. Biography. https://www.biography.com/business-figure/walt-disney
2. Britannica Editors (2025, October 21). Walt Disney | Biography, Films, Company, Characters. Encyclopedia Britannica. https://www.britannica.com/biography/Walt-Disney
3. IMDb (2025, November 10). Walt Disney - Biography. IMDb. https://www.imdb.com/name/nm0227503/bio/
4. Wikipedia Contributors (2001, March 3). Walt Disney. Wikipedia. https://en.wikipedia.org/wiki/Walt_Disney
5. The Walt Disney Company (2025, September 29). About Walt Disney. D23 https://d23.com/walt-disney/
6. JustDisney.com. (North). Walt Disney: A Short Biography. Just Disney. https://justdisney.com/walt-disney-short-biography/

Chapter 6

1. Heartfulness Institute. (2024, January 28). Kamlesh D. Patel (Daaji) Biography. Heartfulness.org. https://heartfulness.org/kamresh-d-patel-daazi/
2. Times of India. (2023, February 2). Kamlesh D. Patel: Spiritual Leader and Heartfulness Guide. Times of India. https://timesofindia.indiatimes.com
3. Wikipedia Contributor. (2006, November 20). -Kamlesh Patel (Daaji). Wikipedia. https://en.wikipedia.org/wiki/Kamlesh_Patel_(Daaji)
4. Daaji.org. (2022, October 25). About Daaji | Spiritual Guide | Rajayoga. Daaji.org. https://daazi.org/about/
5. Stars Unfolded. (2024, March 14). Kamlesh Patel (Daaji) Age, Family, and Biography. Starsunfolded.com. https://starsunfolded.com/kamlesh-patel/
6. Heartfulness. (n.d.). *Heartfulness* [YouTube channel]. YouTube. https://www.youtube.com/@heartfulness

Scan the QR Code for join the AspirixWriters Community

www.ingramcontent.com/pod-product-compliance
Lightning Source LLC
Chambersburg PA
CBHW071521180726
48282CB00058B/705
* 9 7 8 9 3 5 5 2 5 7 3 8 3 *